"Odissi dance is not my profession. It is my identity. It has helped me maintain my self-esteem through the ups and downs of life."

Dr. Rohini Dandavate

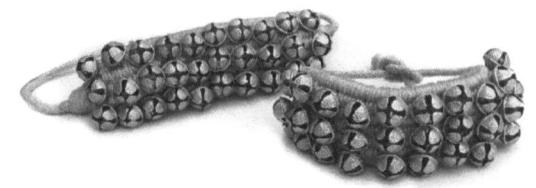

ISBN- 13:978-1541263758
ISBN-10: 1541263758

In memory of
Late Shri. Babulal Doshi

Founder of Kala Vikash Kendra

DANCING, PLAYING & BONDING

IN

KALA VIKASH KENDRA

EDITED BY DR. ROHINI DANDAVATE

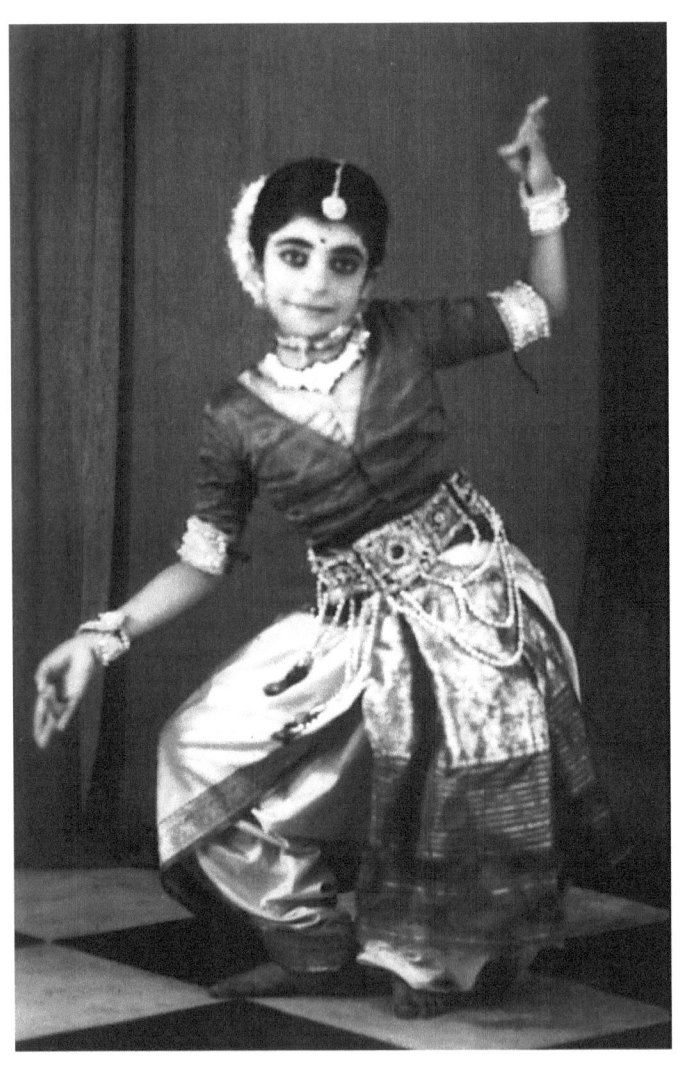

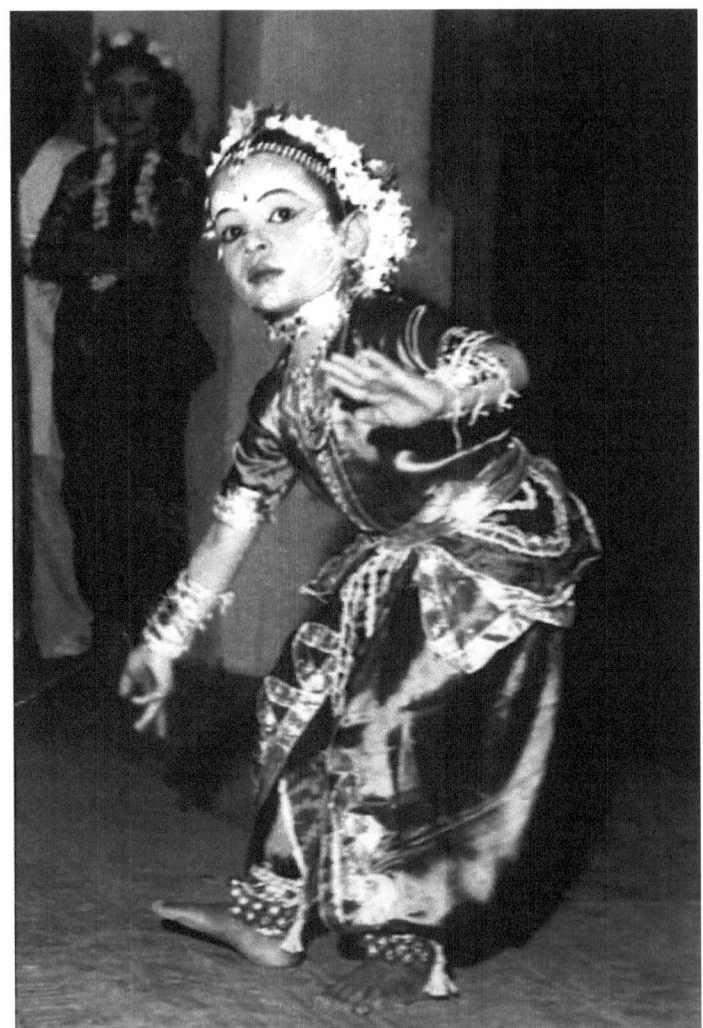

Dr. Nandita Sen   Mrs. Cuckoomeena Das

SINCERE THANKS TO OUR PARENTS FOR INTRODUCING US TO ODISSI DANCE AND KALA VIKASH KENDRA

Nandita Behera: Charubala Das & Subal Chandra Das, **Anita Ray Chowdhury:** Kanak Prava Ray Chowdhury & Dhiren Ray Chowdhury, **Dr. Rohini Doshi Dandavate:** Vijaya Laxmi Doshi & Anantrai Doshi, **Dr. Suchitra Das:** Sudha Manjari Das & Banka Behari Das, **Cuckoomeena Das:** Saila Bala Mohanty & Madhab Charan Mohanty, **Rooplekha Das:** Padmini Ray & Raj Kishore Ray, **Sabita Mishra:** Anasuya Sahu & Baidyanath Sahu, **Prabhat Nalini Misra:** Pramila Das & Padma Charan Das, **Sikata Mohanty:** Kusum Kumari Das & Manoranjan Das, **Pranati Mohanty:** Sharala Parija & Bijan Kumar Parija, **Dr. Sumitra Mohapatra:** Jasodhara Das & Nanda Kumar Das, **Sangeeta Mohapatra Kar:** Beena Mohapatra & Ramakanta Mahapatra, **Tiklimeena Patnaik:** Saila Bala Mohanty & Madhab Charan Mohanty, **Madhu Chhanda Mishra:** Anjelina Pramila Sahu & Debadutta Sahu & Urmila Sahu (Aunt), **Dr. Nandita Sen:** Radha Samuel & Charles Samuel.

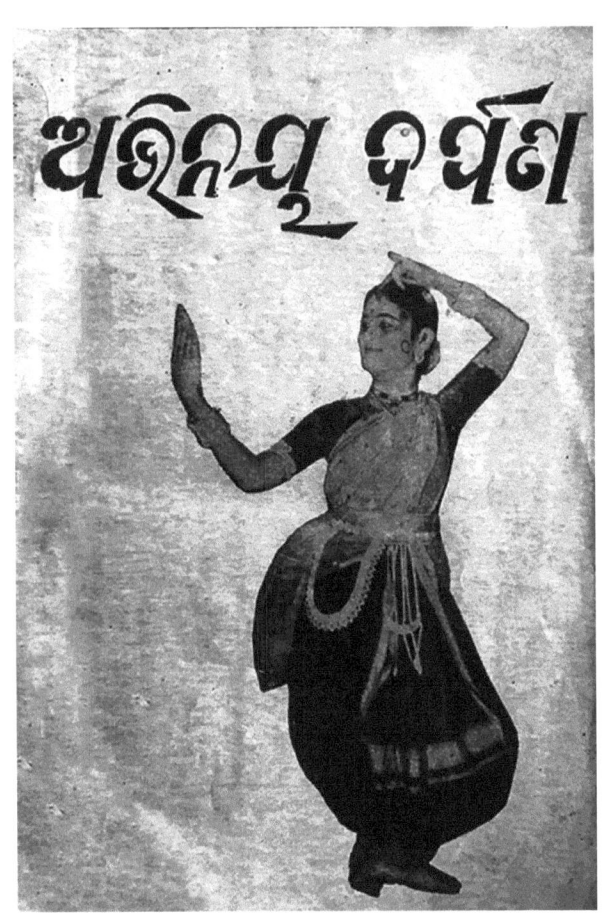
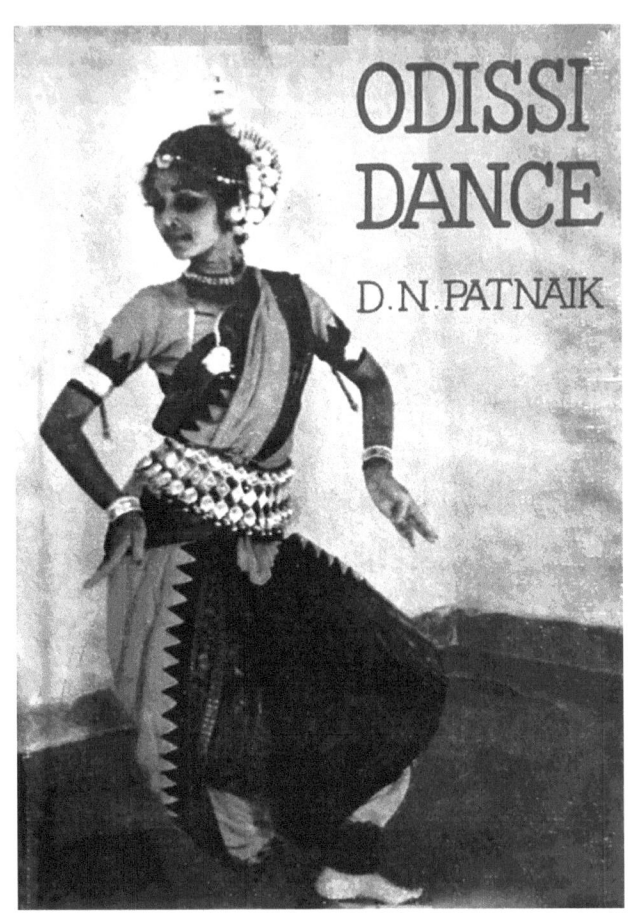

The text books used at KVK

CONTENTS

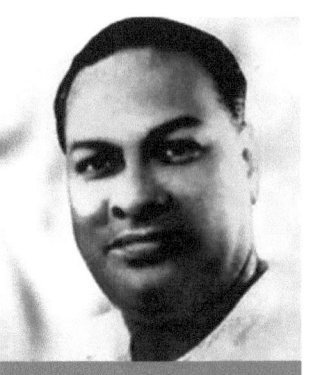

BALAKRUSHNA DAS

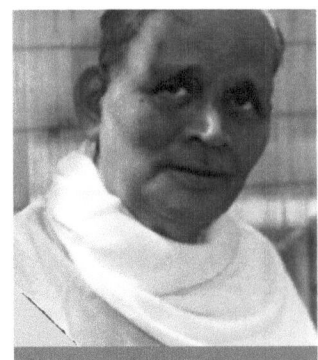

KALICHARAN PATNAIK

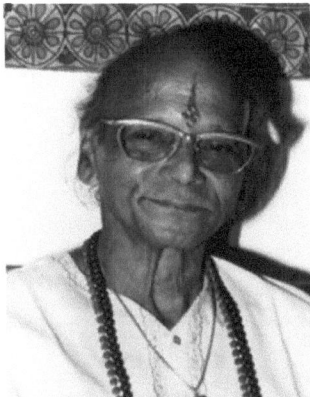

GURU KELUCHARAN MOHAPATRA

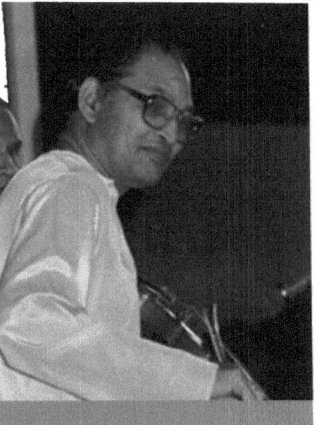

BHUBANESWAR MISRA

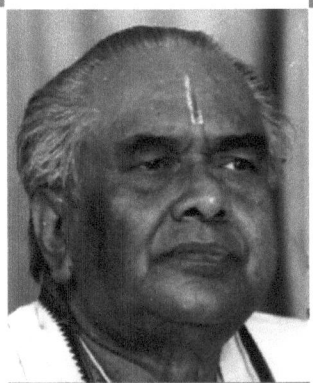

GURU MAYADHAR RAUT

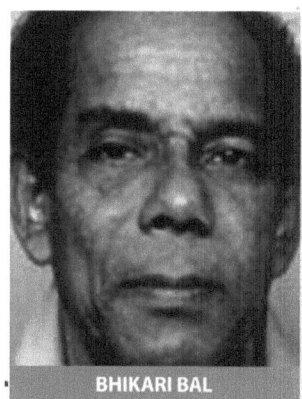

BHIKARI BAL

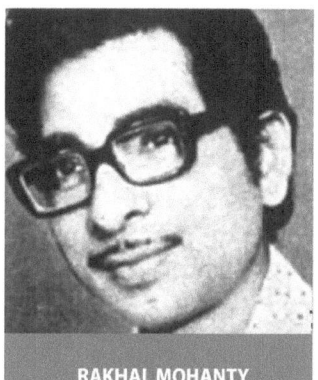

RAKHAL MOHANTY

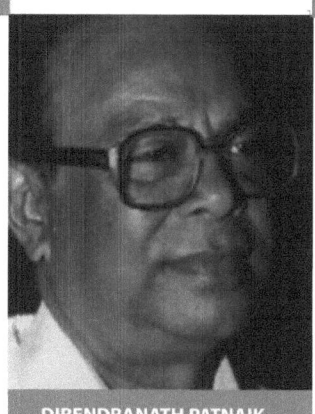

DIRENDRANATH PATNAIK

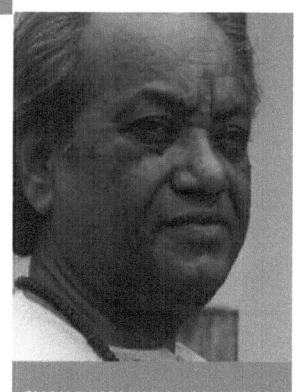

GURU RAMANI RANJAN JENA

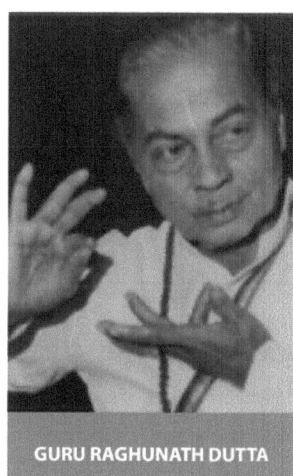

GURU RAGHUNATH DUTTA

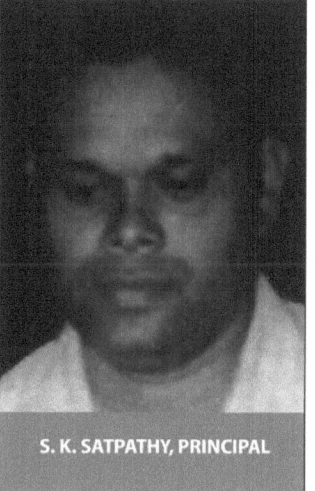

S. K. SATPATHY, PRINCIPAL

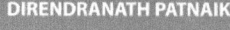

ACKNOWLEDGMENTS

Thanks to all my friends who agreed to share their stories. This book would not have been possible without their contribution.

My deepest gratitude to Babulal Doshi for establishing Kala Vikash Kendra and for dedicating his life to the promotion of the arts. The experiences shared in this book are just one piece of a larger canvas of success stories. I feel blessed to have had the opportunity to participate in his journey and understand his passion, perseverance and indomitable spirit.

Our teachers at KVK were the guiding stars of this journey in our lives. I am indebted to Dr. Menaka Thakkar, Guru Raghunath Dutta, Guru Ramani Ranjan Jena and Guru Kelucharan Mohapatra.

Finally, I would like to thank my family. My parents, who instilled in me the value of dance education and my brothers, Dipak and Bharat, who were with me every step of the way. After getting married, I found a friend in my husband who continues to encourage and support me in all my endeavors. My husband, Uday and my daughter, Isha spent many hours in reviewing this book. Their contribution to my projects of producing learning resources in dance and this book is immense and I will forever remain grateful to them.

EDITOR'S NOTE

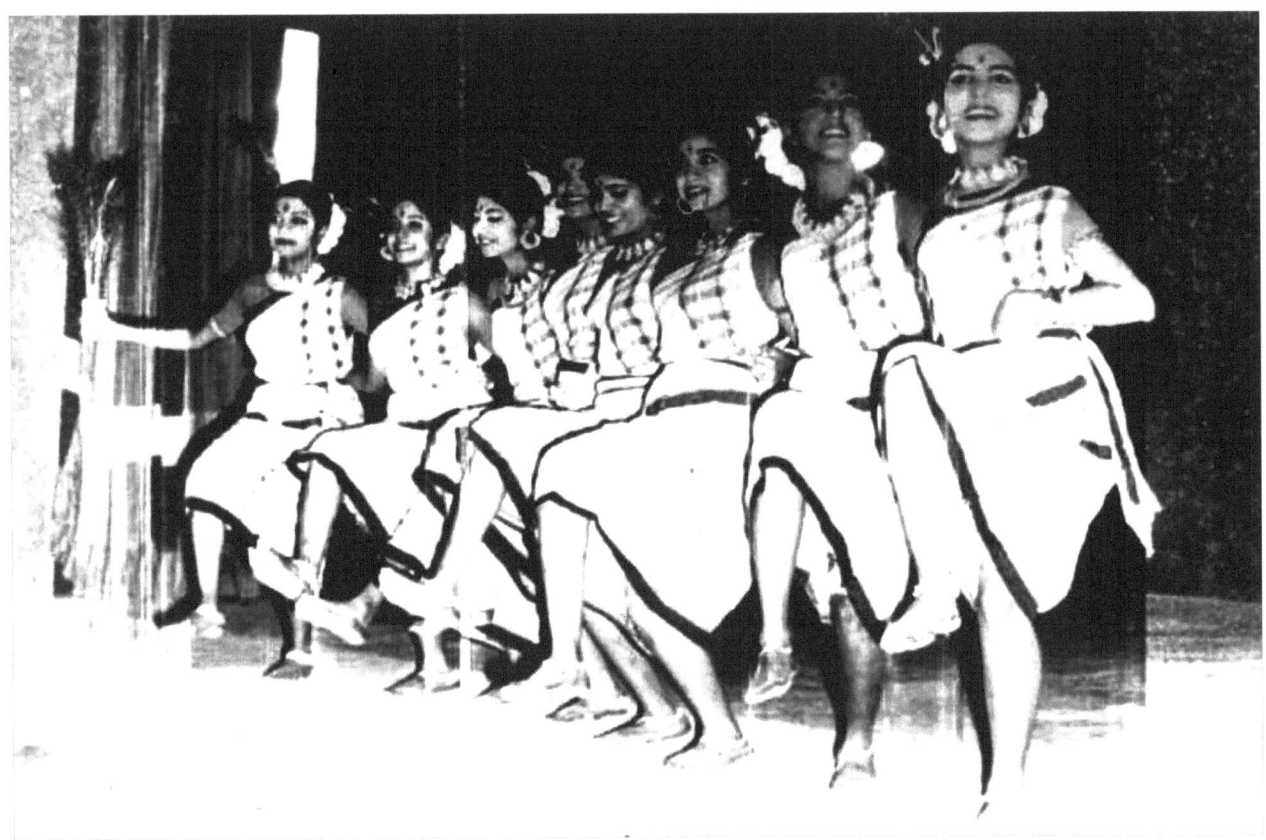

Folk Dance at KVK

This image, posted on Facebook by my friend, Madhu Chhanda, set in motion a viral thread of nostalgic reactions. Within moments of her posting this image, several friends started sharing memories of the beautiful times they had together during 10 to 15 years of learning Odissi at the Kala Vikash Kendra(KVK) in Cuttack. Sensing a fervor amongst my contemporaries to relive those memories, I was inspired to bring together fond memories of the time when we were all students of dance in KVK from the early 60s through the late 70s.

I started learning Odissi at the age of 9 and attending dance classes in KVK became part of my daily schedule. For my parents, learning Odissi dance was as important as my regular classwork at school. At KVK, through the routine and rigor of dance education, we also imbibed important lessons of life. Martha Graham's words, "Dance is just discovery, discovery, discovery" best describes our experience of learning dance, as the beginning of a life full of discoveries. Through dance we discovered our own bodies, found expression for our inner feelings, developed an understanding of the value of teamwork, and above all, made new friends who turned into lifelong relationships. In Kala Vikash Kendra, we danced together, played together, and bonded forever.

This book is a compilation of memories of participating in dance programs, travels, festivals, and the ensuing fun shared by 15 of my contemporaries. Editing these short narratives was a cathartic experience. As we walked down memory lane it became obvious that Odissi dance helped us connect with each other and with other people, made us more disciplined in many aspects of life, and expanded our curiosity and appreciation for the rich diversity of the world. For me this book is a compilation of excerpts from each of our lives, times which gave us joy, camaraderie, and above all an identity and self esteem.

The message I would like to communicate to parents through this book is to introduce children to a dance form. It will make children confident, disciplined, and happy adults and the friendships they develop in the process last a lifetime. They also learn skills which will benefit them in their career in future.

Rohini Dandavate
San Francisco
January 1st, 2017

LATE SHRI BABULAL DOSHI

"The roots below the earth claim no rewards for making the branches fruitful."

- Rabindranath Tagore

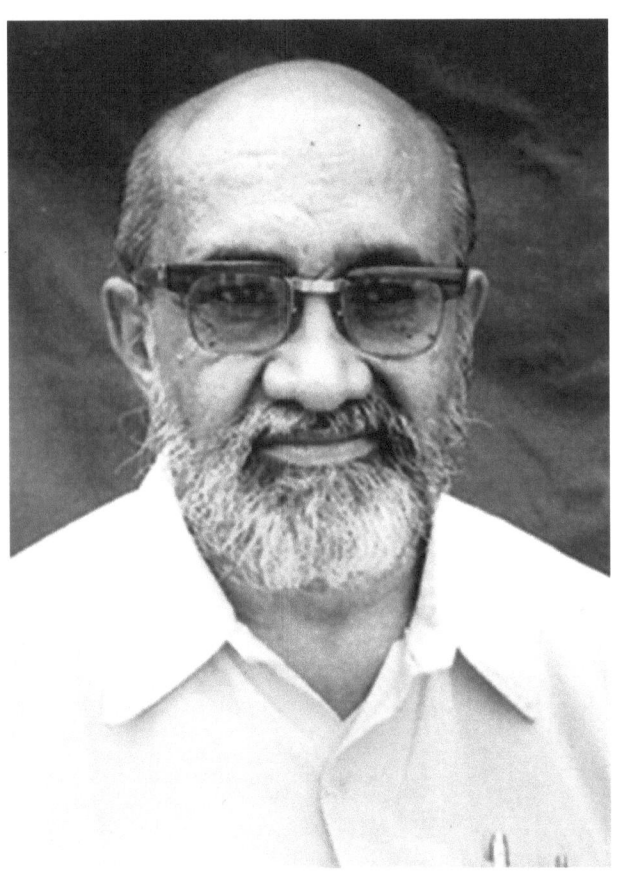

Late Shri Babulal Doshi, the founder of Kala Vikash Kendra (KVK) was Babu kaka (uncle) to me. Though it was my mother who initiated my pursuit in Odissi dance education, it was Babu Kaka's inimitable and unconditional support through the years which led me to discover the true joy of dance. Babu Kaka's KVK was a College of dance, music and theater where stalwarts like Bhikhari Chandra Bal, Rakhal Mohanty, Pundit Bhubaneswar Mishra, Guru Kelucharan Mohapatra, Guru Raghunath Dutta and Guru Ramani Ranjan trained students in various disciplines of the arts. I was privileged to be able to learn and grow in this institution under the tutelage of legendary gurus.

As I look back various images of Babu Kaka come to mind. One could not miss his towering personality with resolute determination to pursue his dreams. As a kid, I would see a black car pulling in front of our cycle shop and soon Babu Kaka accompanied by his lifelong friend Bai bhai, would emerge from it. It was understood that he was visiting to check about my progress in dance training besides giving us an update on Kendra's ongoing and upcoming activities and how we could contribute. For years this was a routine. Many a times he would catch me in the corridors of KVK and enquire about my progress in class. I was often invited to his home for lunch and Shanta Kaki, his wife would have a spread of delicious dishes laid out on the dining table. As a twelve year old, dancing in his film Adina Megha, was another opportunity to explore and learn about what it takes to participate in movies.

A true visionary, his lifelong quest was to promote, propagate and preserve the rich art forms of Odisha. He spent his entire life for this cause. Young in age, I never understood his passion. I often wondered what inspired him to dedicate his entire life for the arts of Odisha, especially because it was not a normal pursuit for a traditional Gujarati businessman, who also was once the treasurer of the Socialist Party in Odisha. He recognized the value of the arts in human development and his invincible spirit would leave no stones unturned to bring the rich heritage of Odisha to the forefront. John Barth, from the Floating Opera once said, "Nothing is intrinsically valuable; the value of everything is attributed to it, assigned to it from outside the thing itself, by people (1956). Babu Kaka, was one such person who understood the value of the arts and was determined to build an institution which would work towards preserving and taking Odisha's tradition of dance, music and theatre beyond its boundaries.

His public relations, networking, and marketing skills were extraordinary. Though not formally trained in the art of business management the professionalism he displayed in his work was no different from the methods taught to students of business management.

His regular visits to potential individual donors; corporations, media representatives and officials of government organizations were an effort in expanding his reach, network and create visibility. Students of KVK traveled far and wide in India to showcase their art. Intensive Odissi dance workshops were held during summer holidays, to attract dancers from other states and abroad. Many a times he invited scholars, researchers and gurus from different parts of India to give students of KVK an opportunity to experience diverse art forms and understand new perspectives. Alongside the classical art forms, the folk traditions of Orissa were taught and showcased during various festivals. The theatre unit was equally active in presenting dramas. Residential facilities were built for students, Gurus and working women who came from other parts of Odisha and needed a living place. A library was also set up in the premises. In a short span of time KVK became the hub of all artistic activity and came to be recognized as the premier institute for the arts in Odisha.

Prof G.T. Smith, professor of Rhetoric and Philosophy, once said, "Donors don't give to institutions. They invest in ideas and people in whom they believe". Sponsors, patrons of the arts, gurus, government officials and media representatives recognized the capacity of the Babulal Doshi and his team. He gained the trust and confidence of people from the field of the arts nationally and from the larger local community. He received support in all forms and was successful in fulfilling his life long dream. During the last years of his life he vowed to wear no footwear and live with the bare minimum necessities and focus upon meeting the infrastructural and financial goals of KVK. His fund raising campaign started in 1952, when Kala Vikash Kendra was first established and continued until his death in 1986.

KALA VIKASH KENDRA

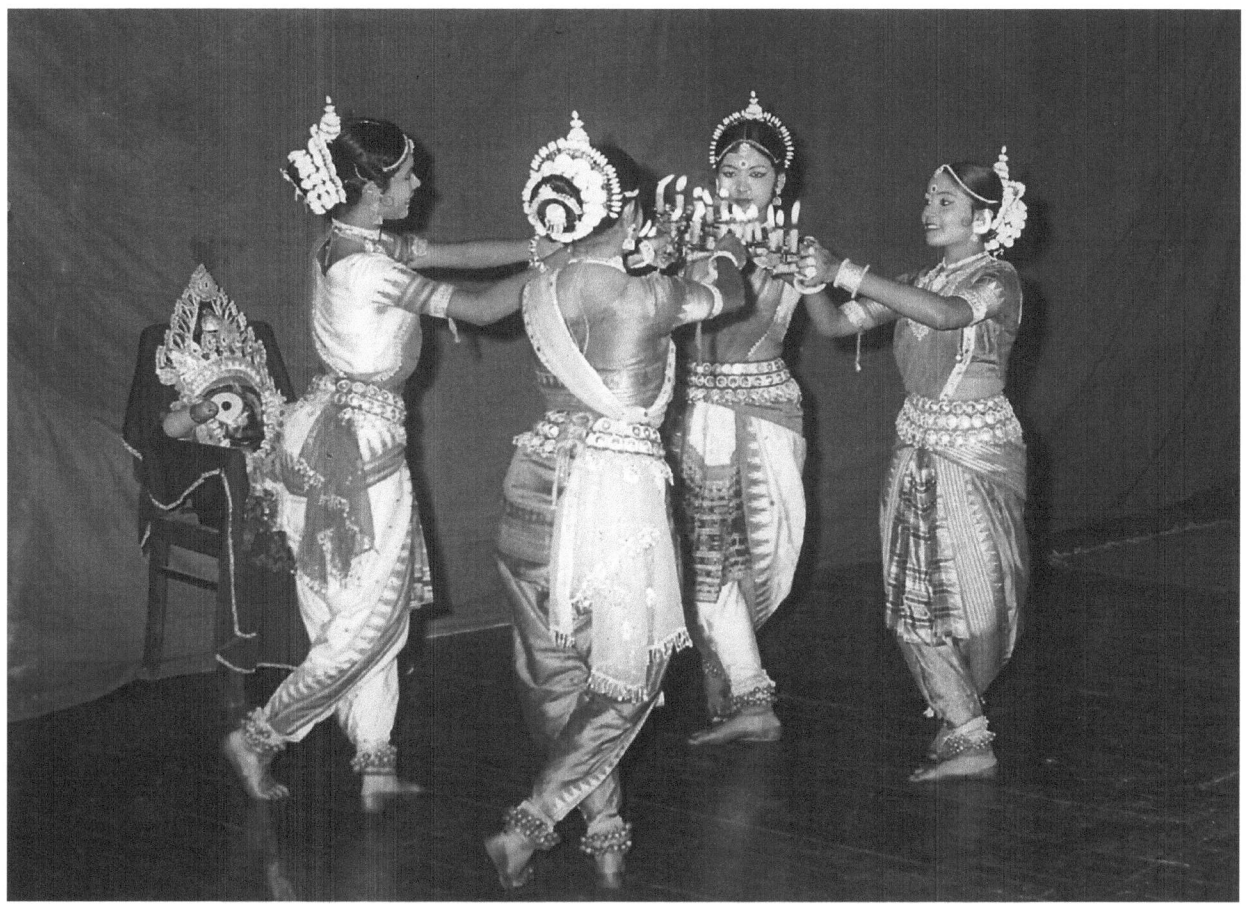

Odissi Performance at The Lal Bahadur Shastri National Academy of Administration, Mussoorie

Kala Vikash Kendra in Cuttack, popularly known as KVK was established on 10th August, 1952. After India received independence from the British Rule, there was a thrust by the Government of India to revive, restore and promote the arts of India all over the country. Babulal Doshi, an immigrant to Odisha and the treasurer of the Socialist Party in Odisha took over the monumental task of propagating the arts of Odisha. He dreamt big and dedicated his life to establish an institution, which can become the main hub for dancers, musicians, theater personalities and scholars to work, teach and nurture artistic traditions of Odisha.

Initially KVK was housed in a rented space in Banka Bazar, Cuttack. In a span of six years, Babulal Doshi travelled far and wide introducing Odissi dance in other parts of India and raising funds for the institution as he had envisioned. With the help of leading politicians, media representatives, social workers and local patrons he finally laid the foundation of his dream College of the arts, Kala Vikash Kendra in the year 1958 when Dr. Harekrushna Mahtab, the Chief Minister of Odisha allotted a land for the institution. The ground level of the building was inaugurated by Humanyun Kabir, the Central Minister for Education in the year 1959, followed by the completion of the first level of the building in 1960 and inaugurated by Smt. Kamala Devi Chattopadhyay. In the year 1977, the Silver Jubilee Celebrations of KVK was held in the new auditorium, inaugurated by the Vice President of India, Shri B.D. Jatti.

Since its inception KVK, under the able leadership of Babulal Doshi and his team of passionate and hard working staff expanded its purview by offering degree courses in dance, music and theater. It drew legendary gurus, scholars from the field of arts and curriculum for formal education in various disciplines was developed. KVK was affiliated to the Akhil Bharatiya Gandharva Mahavidyalaya Mandal, Maharastra and Orissa Sangeet Natak Akademi. The curriculum developed in KVK was a pioneering effort in the study of Odissi dance. The history of arts and culture in Odisha would remain incomplete without the mention of Babulal Doshi and KVK.

CHAPTER ONE

NANDITA BEHERA

"Everything in the Universe has rhythm. Everything dances."
- Maya Angelou

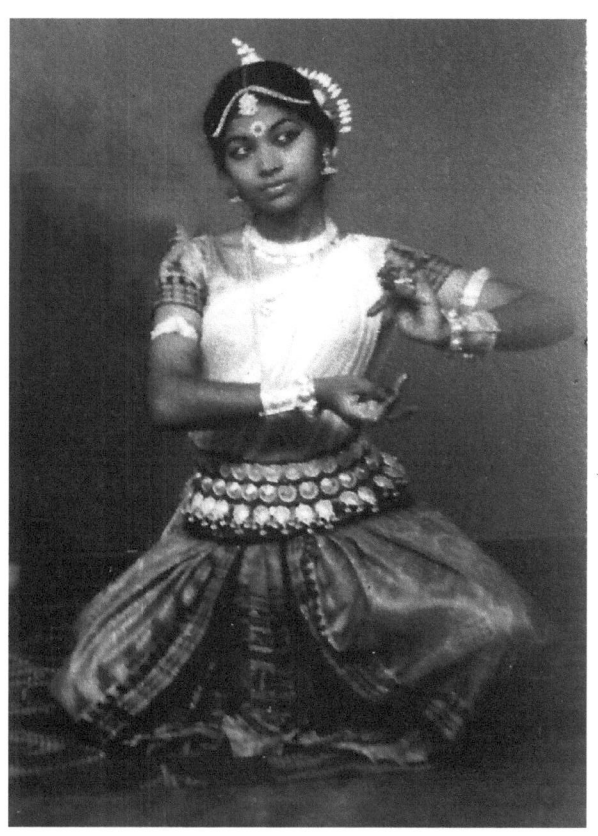

I began learning Odissi dance at a very young age. In the year 1969, I saw a performance by Smt. Sanjukta Panigrahi for the first time in a small town called Bhadrak in Odisha. Watching Sanjukta Panigrahi on stage ignited a fire inside me. I was curious to meet the creator of this wonderful dance style. Within a week my father dropped me off to Kala Vikash Kendra.

As a teenager I soon forgot my little home and my family as I entered this magical world of dance and music. During that time, KVK was the Mecca of this art form. It was the only vibrant institution offering music and dance education programs in Odisha. It was the hub of arts-related activities and it was here that dance gurus like Kelucharan Mohapatra, Raghunath Dutta, Ramani Ranjan Jena, and other senior dancers, scholars, and singers used to teach. We watched Guruji choreograph innumerable Odissi dance numbers and dance dramas. Memories of our summer classes conducted by senior dancers under the direct supervision of Guruji are still clear in my mind.

I started my initial training under Guru Raghunath Dutta, a soft-spoken teacher with a sweet smile. It was in

KVK where I met my dance sisters. One of my most interesting experience was participating in Kumar Utsav Festival and rehearsals. We camped there through the day and night and watched Guruji choreograph a different dance drama each ensuing year. More than dancing I was interested in spending time with my sister-like friends, sharing treats and tea together. We were amidst pundits of the field, namely Bhubaneswar Mishra, Raghunath Panigrahi, Balakrushna Das, Bhikari Bala, and Rakhal Mohanty, the pioneers in Odissi music. We were like sponges, unconsciously soaking in the experience of dance making and singing. We were all playing in a dreamland of graceful dance and beautiful music.

Each year during my training in KVK, our group had the opportunity to go on dance tours to different parts of India as cultural ambassadors of Odisha. I feel humbled each time I think of Mr. Babulal Doshi, the founder of KVK. He was a visionary and even though he was not a native of Odisha he spent his life propagating and promoting the arts of Odisha. Today, as I look back and reminisce about the countless hours I spent with all the great gurus, and the precious knowledge I received, I recognize the role KVK played in my life. While I continue to teach Odissi dance in the US and am now addressed as Guru, I feel indebted to this institution where I started my humble journey many years back as a teenager.

CHAPTER TWO

ANITA RAY CHOWDHURY

"The dancers body is simply the luminous manifestation of the soul."
- Isadora Duncan

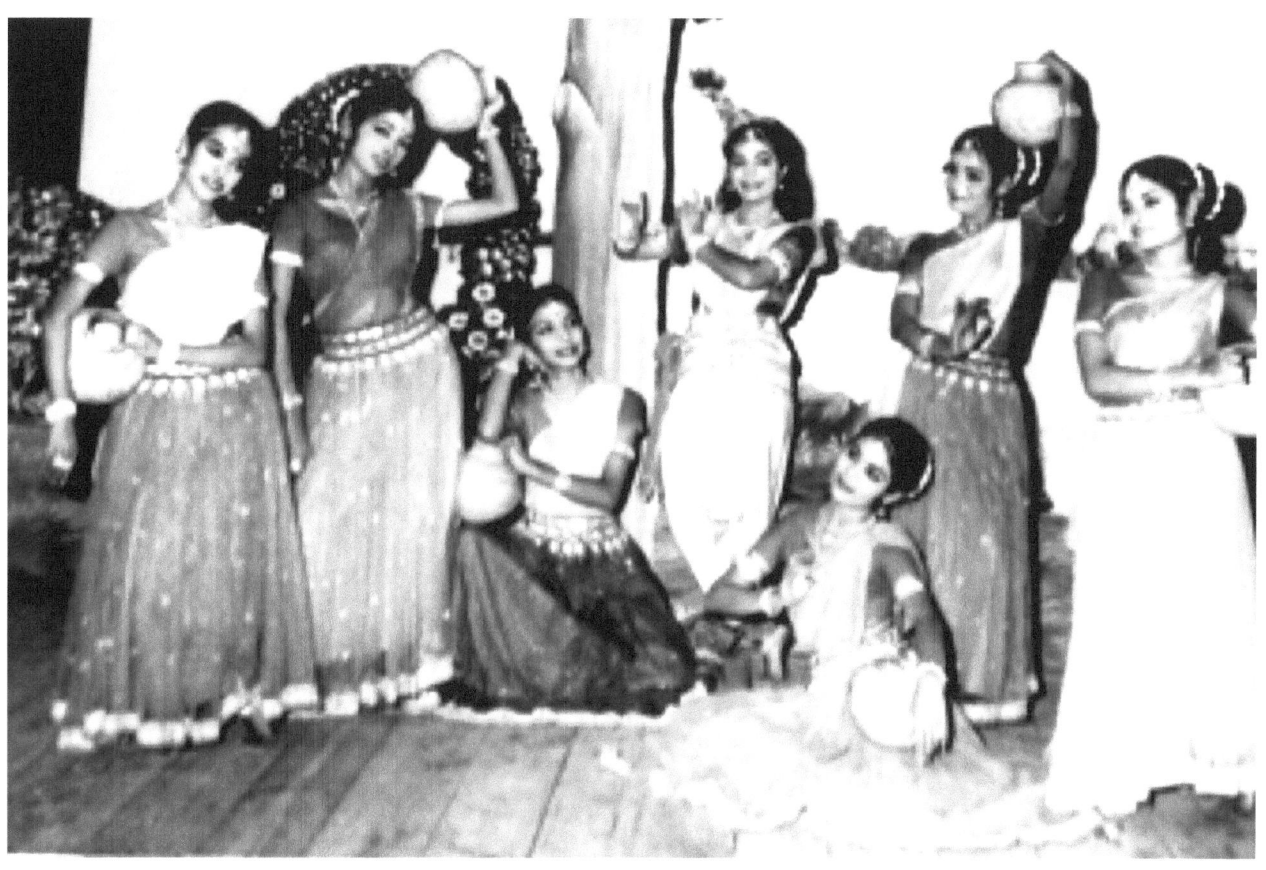

Anita (extreme right) in the dance drama Krishna Gatha

I started attending Odissi dance classes at Kala Vikash Kendra, Cuttack with my younger sister, Mamata when I was around 5 years old and since then dance has continued to be my passion. As I think of those times, I remember that in Prarambhik, the elementary level class, our first guru was late Raghunath Dutta. We learned the basic steps in Chowk and Tribhangi, Mudras, and Bhangis.

From the 4th year of our training, our teachers were Guru Ramani Ranjan Jena, and Guru Kelu Charan Mohapatra. After seven years of regular practice and dedication to complete the Odissi dance course, we attended four years of an intensive course offered every summer by our beloved Kelu Sir. Among all the dance numbers we learned in our curriculum, my favorite dances are Dasavatar, Batu, Aravi & Basant Pallavi, Yahi Madhava, Vadasi Yadi Kinchidapi in Abhinaya, and Namami Bighnaraja Twang, the Mangalacharan.

During my training in KVK, I had the opportunity to participate in several festivals, performances, and dance tours. As I think about those experiences, I feel I collected a heart full of happy memories with some dear friends, which I cherish the most from that phase in my life. Learning Odissi dance in KVK was an enriching experience.

A very special story to share is when in Prarambhik, our Kelu Sir was teaching a class in the dance hall and I hid behind the doors to watch the dance of the famous dancer Smt. Ranikarna. Kelu sir saw me and called me over. I was very nervous. However, Sir made me comfortable and asked, "Do you want to be a good Odissi dancer like her?" I instantly nodded my head with affirmation. Sir smiled and replied, "You have to learn with complete dedication" and those words became my mantra. This memory still brings a smile to my face.

This journey of learning Odissi dance in KVK, is one of the most beautiful experiences of my life and is part of my soul. The perfection of Late Sanju Nani (Smt. Sanjukta Panigrahi), inspired me. Thanks Rohini for bringing all our friends from KVK together again, and making this effort to relive those days. Revisiting that time and sharing my experience of learning dance in KVK has definitely brightened my life even more and makes me feel young again.

CHAPTER THREE

DR. ROHINI DANDAVATE

"You have to love dancing to stick to it. It gives you nothing back, no manuscripts, no paintings, no poems, nothing but that single fleeting moment when you feel alive."

- Merce Cunningham

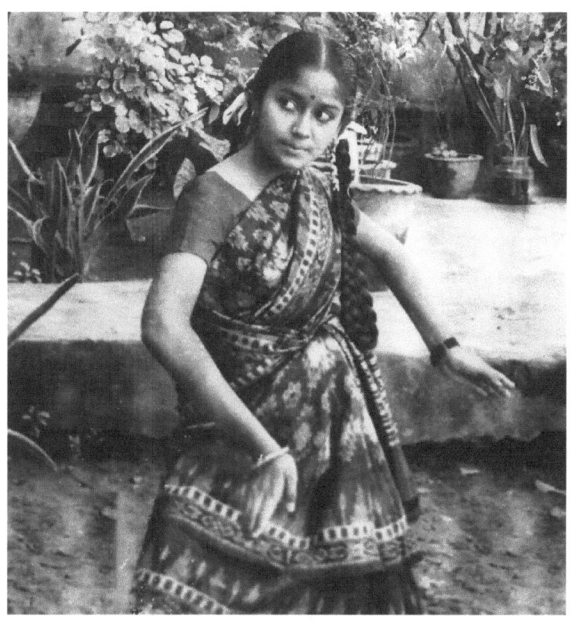

Reminiscing the days and years I spent learning Odissi dance in KVK brings alive images of many moments. The reverberating sound of mardal playing and music in the corridors, the rickshaw rides to KVK from home, the chitchatting and laughter with friends and climbing the guava trees in Nandita Sen's home across KVK and many more. Kala Vikash Kendra holds a special place in my heart.

Odissi dance introduced me to the Odiya culture, language, and literature. My parents were natives of Gujarat and had migrated to Cuttack for work. Though at home we lived the traditional Gujarati lifestyle and spoke the Gujarati language, in KVK, I got the opportunity to delve into the culture of the state in which I was born and experience the rich heritage. It was cultural immersion to the fullest during the 15 years of training.

My mother introduced me to dance at the age of 9. My first instructor was Dr. Menaka Thakkar, one of the leading Bharat Natyam dancers who visited KVK from Mumbai to be trained in Odissi dance under Guru Kelucharan Mohapatra. In a span of few months, Dr. Thakkar trained me in the basics of Odissi as taught in the Prarambhik (elementary) class. On passing my exams that year I was admitted to the regular six year long course in Odissi dance education and since then, my journey in dance continues. Over the years, my career path has included areas of dance performance, arts administration, dance education, cultural policy, and dance research.

Learning Odissi dance shaped my life. By developing the qualities I needed to pursue the study of Odissi dance, I imbibed many other skill sets required for achieving success in life. While the rigor of dance practice contributed to my fitness, coordinating dance postures and movements of different parts of the body aided in identifying my physical limitations. The discipline of being on time for classes and performances taught me the importance of punctuality. Collaboration with other dancers helped me build an understanding of teamwork. Knowledge of costumes, sets, and lighting groomed my imagination and aesthetics. The process of learning dance nurtured these competencies which later in my professional career facilitated collaboration, self-accountability, self-awareness and awareness of others and problem solving.

Numerous travels for dance programs became opportunities to connect with different kinds of people. Furthermore, the experience of performing for unfamiliar audiences was a challenge, and each time it was a unique experience. We enjoyed the attention we received from people different from us. Our dance tours took us to Calcutta, Shantiniketan, Madras, New Delhi, Bangalore, Mysore, Hyderabad, Vijaywada, Vishakhapatnam, Etawah, Guwahati, Shillong, and to many other parts of Odisha. The highlight of our travels was visiting the tourist attractions in every city and trying out the cuisines of those places.

My list of fond memories is long and I cannot possibly share all. I can only say that KVK, Babulal Doshi and my Gurus have left an everlasting imprint on me. Odissi dance is my identity and I feel blessed to have had the opportunity to spend the precious years of my childhood and youth in this institution.

CHAPTER FOUR

DR. SUCHITRA DAS

"In art, Man reveals himself and not his objects."
-Rabindranath Tagore

It was the summer of 1972. The blissful afternoon breaks were spent plucking guavas. Guavas were more desirable because they were from the neighboring property. All the more reason- eating the fruit was prohibited by Guruji during practice classes. And we were not the most obedient teenagers. The 20 minute breaks during the summer classes were great to catch up on gossip, to steal guavas and eat as much pickle as possible. All these things were a strict no-no in Guruji's class. Guruji was indeed a taskmaster. His strict discipline and time management later on became an integral part of my life despite being away from the field of Odissi for many decades now. Where else could all these lessons of life be imparted along with Odissi training- Kala Vikash Kendra, Cuttack and who else could teach us all of it other than Padmavibhusan Guru Kelu Charan Mohapatra.

I became a part of KVK in the early months of '67 and continued till the end of '71 and then joined the summer classes in the year '72 and '73. Vivid memories of 'Circus'- a dance drama- makes me smile even after 45 years. Rohini and I along with two more were circus girls while Salila and Srikant Nanda played the role of the jokers. No less was an overnight bus journey to Rourkela for a dance performance, which broke down early in the morning before we could reach our destination. While the bus was being repaired few of us wandered to a nearby stream and had the time of our life splashing around in the water until we were called back to join with the rest of the group. We boarded a truck to Redhakol and stayed in the Inspection Bungalow for the whole day.

One of the many incidents that pulls the strings of nostalgia from deep within is the shooting of "Adina Megha". Mr. Babulal Doshi, being such a gentleman, had called my parents to take permission before signing me up for the dance shoot and took extreme care of me as I was unwell. The movie production team along with the KVK group was put up at the staff quarters of Daitari mines. That was the first time I had ever seen so many roses in full bloom. The day long shooting used to keep us occupied while the winter evenings were spent in playing badminton. Recently I saw the song sequence from the movie and attempted recognizing my co dancers. To my surprise, even after so many years I did recognize all my friends.

Apart from such priceless memories, KVK was a platform to interact with eminent artists and writers like Kabichandra Kalicharan Patnaik (who was the external faculty in 4th year practical examination). My Odissi foundation was laid by Guru Raghunath Dutta and I was also taught by Guru Ramani Ranjan Jena. Being a part of KVK, not only made me a better dancer but shaped me as a complete human being.

CHAPTER FIVE

CUCKOOMEENA DAS

"Dancers are the athletes of God."
Albert Einstein

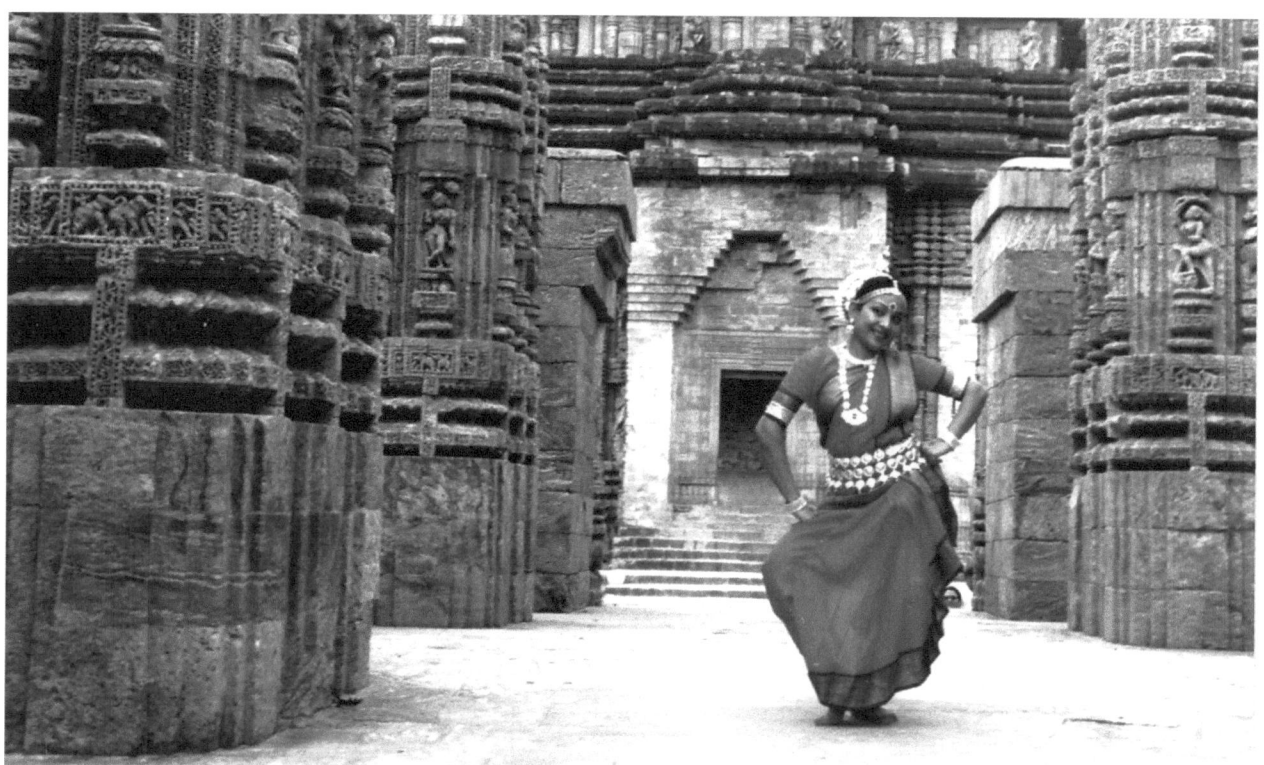

The memories of my childhood are still fresh in my mind. Today, as I sit to write about my experience of learning dance, I am reminded of my deep association with my dance school, Kala Vikash Kendra.

When I was around two and a half years old, my parents noticed my keen interest in dance and they decided to arrange for someone to teach me dance at home. Guru Kelu Charan Mohapatra agreed to fulfill the request of my parents, and my journey in learning Odissi dance began. It was in second or third grade when I took admission in KVK for dance theory lessons. My association with KVK began and attending classes became a part and parcel of my life.

In those days our dance school was in

a rented house at Banka Bazar, Cuttack. Babulal Doshi was trying to get a good space for KVK and get it accredited as a recognized institution at the national level. Other staff members, namely Raghunath Dutta, Nilamadhab Bose, Ganesh, Chandra Babu and many others were also working towards the development of KVK.

KVK was quite far from my house and because of this, I had to discontinue the course in the third year of my training. That did not stop me from learning dance. I resumed learning at home, this time from Guru Raghunath Dutta. However, often I was invited by KVK to participate in dance tours in and out of the state.

KVK was like a second home, because everybody took great care of us when we travelled. We never felt home sick. Train reservations were made well in advance so that we could travel comfortably. Kelu Sir (Guruji), as he was lovingly addressed, personally supervised the minute details of all our needs. In those days the berths in the compartments were not padded. Therefore Guruji took extra care in arranging the bed by joining the boxes (metallic) we carried in those days & spread our beddings over them, so that we could sleep comfortably. Guruji would get up multiple times in

the middle of the night to ensure our safety and would cover us by tucking bed sheets tightly so that we would not fall off the bed. I used to sleep until quite late in the morning deliberately because I did not like to sit for a long time in the train. In the morning, Guruji would come and affectionately ask me to wake up, brush my teeth and have breakfast as other friends had already finished their breakfast. Babu bhai (Babulal Doshi) always brought ganthia and bundi in large biscuit containers. We all anxiously waited every morning to be served with Babu bhai's special snacks, which were absolutely delicious.

In due course, Babu bhai's dream was fulfilled when the construction of KVK's own building was completed. Babulal Doshi had vowed to not use footwear, eat on a leaf instead of a plate, and sleep on the ground till the building was complete. His dedication and sincerity is praiseworthy, especially as he was an immigrant to Odisha and yet dedicated his life to promoting the arts of Odisha. Recognizing his determination, many new members like Pratap babu, Mayadhar babu, Abani Kumar Roy, Baikunth Nath Mohanty & others came forward and joined him to help in the advancement of KVK.

In 1972 I joined the summer course

under the guidance of Guruji. The classes used to start by nine a.m. & continued till one p.m. Then we would break for the lunch and resume class from three p.m. to seven p.m. This training helped me to build endurance and develop expertise in performing for more than two hours. I was fortunate enough to receive valuable tips from Raghu Sir, Mayadhar Sir (Guru Mayadhar Raut), and Nilu Da (Nila Madhab Bose). Many dancers like Ramani Ranjan Jena, Menaka Thakkar (An eminent Bharat Natyam dancer from Mumbai), Nandita Samuel, Natabar Moharana and many others attended the class and we all spent time together like one big family. We used to cook khichdi (a typical Oriya delicacy made of dal, rice, and vegetables) on Menaka Di's stove in her hostel room. I cannot forget how we all enjoyed and relished it. Ramani's family was staying in KVK campus at that time, so we would cook at his residence too and would sit and eat together. This was indeed another unique experience. We bonded forever. I completed two years of my summer course. I often performed in various places of India and abroad as a cultural ambassador.

After my marriage I moved to Bhubaneswar and my visits to KVK decreased, but I was still contacted for programs. Learning Odissi dance and participating in numerous dance performances added immense joy to my life and I am truly grateful to my teachers, friends and associates at KVK. Their love, guidance, and care will always be cherished and continue to inspire me to this day. I treasure those beautiful days that we spent together in Kala Vikash Kendra.

CHAPTER SIX

ROOPLEKHA DAS

"Learning to walk sets you free. Learning to dance gives you the greatest freedom of all: to express with your whole self, the person you are."

- Melissa Hayden

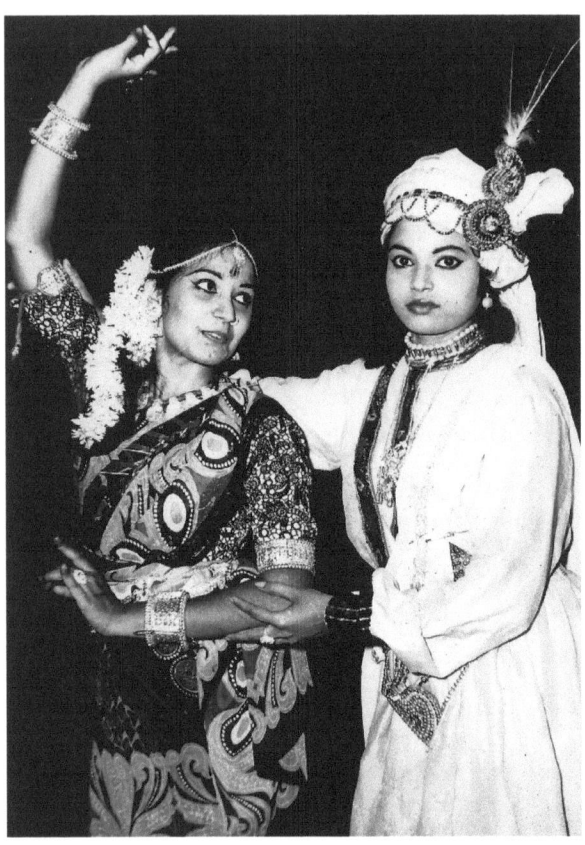

Rooplekha (right) with Rohini (left) in "Srikhetra"

I began learning Odissi dance sometime in the years 1962 or 1963. Along with so many friends I spent almost a decade in this training and also attended the intensive summer classes. In the elementary stage of our dance studies, we were trained by Raghu sir, Ramani Sir, or sometimes Mayadhar Sir, and it was only in the senior years when we took lessons from Guru Kelucharan Mohapatra.

Raghu Sir taught us the basic steps in Odissi and the mudras. We learned Abhinayas and Pallavis from Ramani Sir. Kelu Sir was the choreographer of the various dance dramas we participated in. My training with Mayadhar Sir lasted only for few months only because he moved out of State to New Delhi.

As a young student I enjoyed watching Guru Kelu Sir while he was choreographing for shows. Due to his deep involvement in dance making, he almost forgot himself and worked late hours in the process. He worked endlessly, dedicating one hundred percent of himself to producing a perfect dance number which could appeal to everyone. He was a man of amazing integrity, with unique teaching skills, and it was a privilege to learn from him. As students of dance since childhood, we learned to follow a disciplined and dedicated lifestyle. Though I discontinued my training in dance after 1976 to pursue other interests, it was the skills I gained as a dancer which helped me win awards and earn national acclaim.

My sincere thanks to my gurus and to Kala Vikash Kendra for providing me the space, opportunity, and resources to develop a skill set that opened many other windows of opportunity in my professional career.

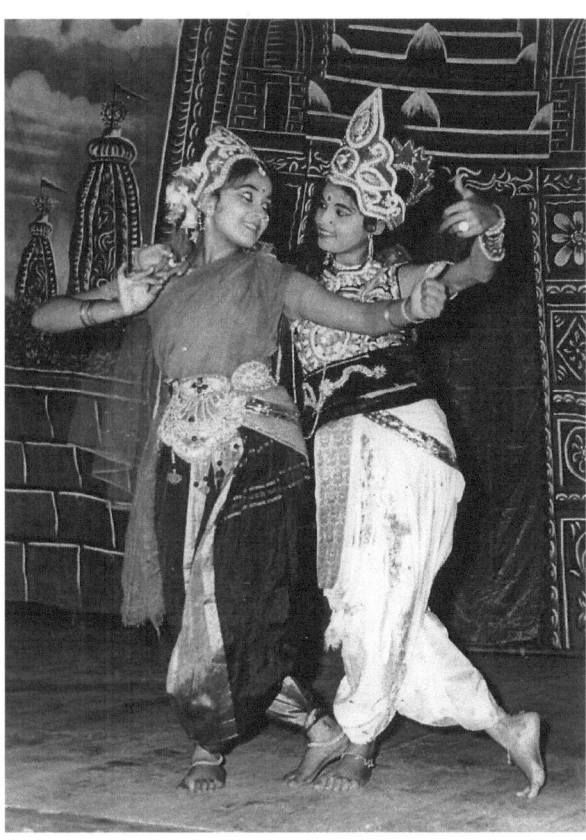

Rooplekha (right) with Rohini (left) in " Srikhetra"

CHAPTER SEVEN

MADHU CHHANDA MISHRA

"In Art, man reveals himself and not his objects."
-Rabindranath Tagore

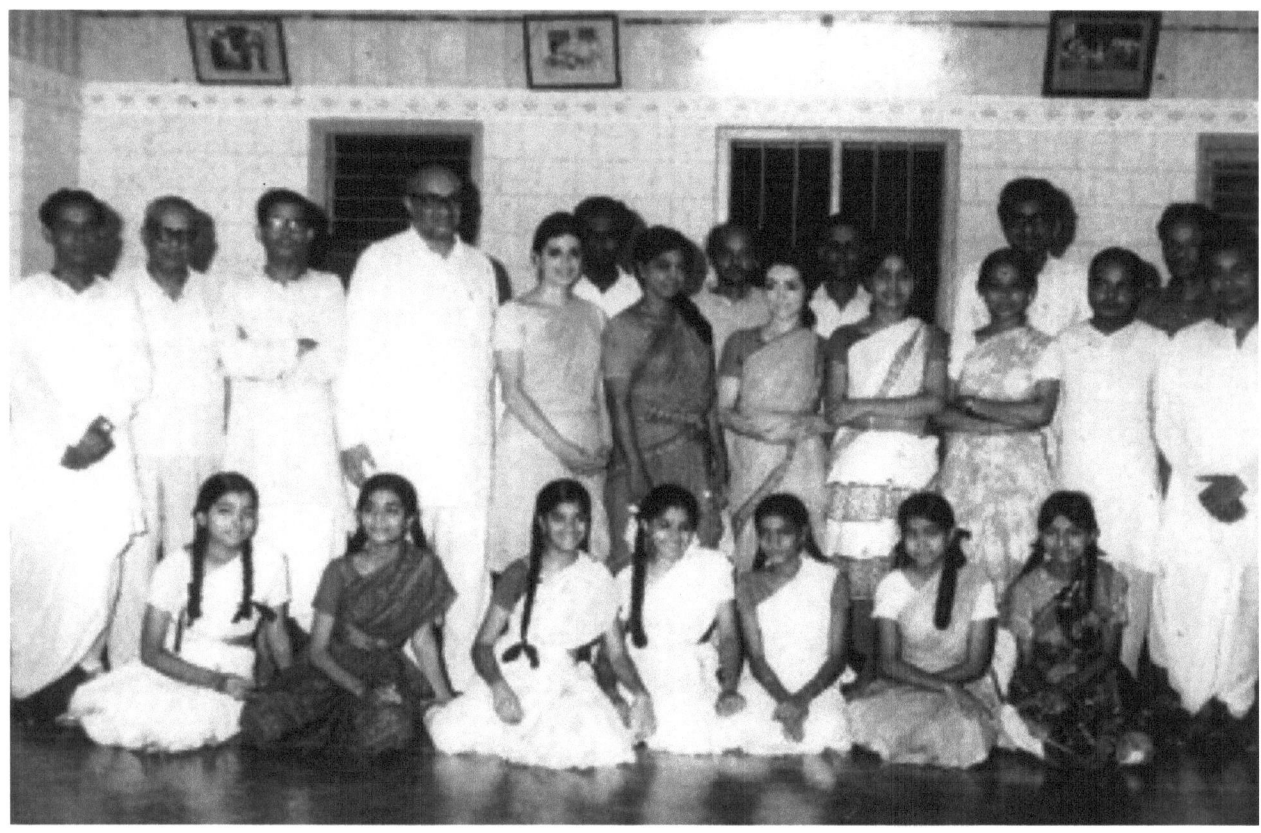

Madhu Chhanda (seated second from right) with attendees and faculty of summer workshop.

In the year 1964, when I was six years old I joined Kala Vikash Kendra in Prarambhik class of Odissi Dance, and my learning continued for the next fourteen years. My first imprint of Odissi dance was through Guru Raghunath Dutta. Like many of my friends, I too learned the basic steps from him. In the senior grade, Guru Ramani Ranjan Jena contributed a lot in teaching me different Abhinayas (expressive dances) alongside other numbers of the Odissi repertoire. As far as my memory goes, Guru Mayadhar Raut also had been my mentor for few months only but I cherished his teaching. After completing seven years of rigorous training, I even joined summer classes, where Guru Kelu Charan Mohapatro became my mentor.

The co-operation and dedication of my mentors enabled me to establish myself as a Odissi dancer within and beyond the state. The regular classes and the long arduous practice to the beat of mardal is still unforgettable.

Mr. Babulal Doshi, the founder of Kala Vikash Kendra, my lifelong mentor, was a great supporter of Odissi dance and music. He encouraged and supported us in pursuing the study of dance and music. As a group we performed many times and even travelled out of the state.

Besides learning dance, I also learned Odissi music. Guru Bhikari Bala and Guru Rakhal Chandra Mohanty were my teachers then. However, because my focus was on dance, I discontinued learning music after pursuing it for about five years. Though many of my Gurus are no more, I will always be indebted to them for their contribution in building my career as an Odissi dancer. KVK holds a special place in my heart and I treasure the memories of all the beautiful experiences KVK provided to us.

Even though at present I am working as a Senior English teacher in one of the renowned schools of Cuttack, I have not forgotten my steps and I continue to utilize my talent and experience as a dancer and train the students in my institution.

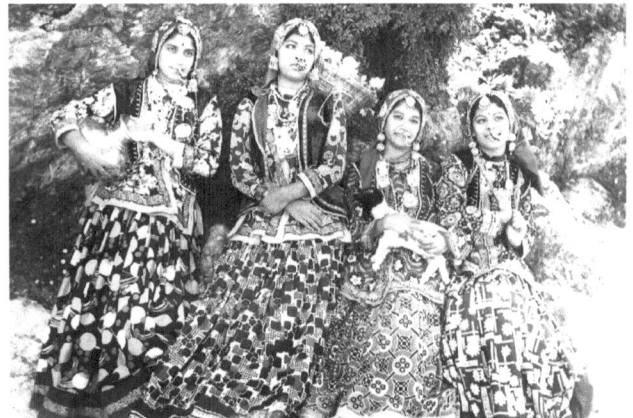

Dressing up in a local fair in Mussoorie

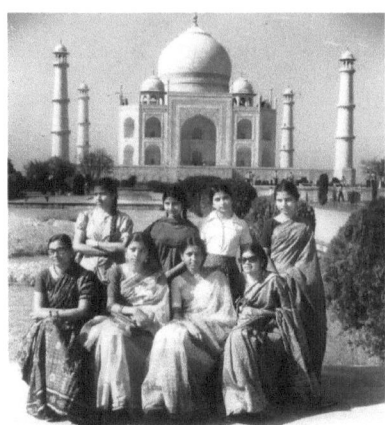

A visit to Taj Mahal

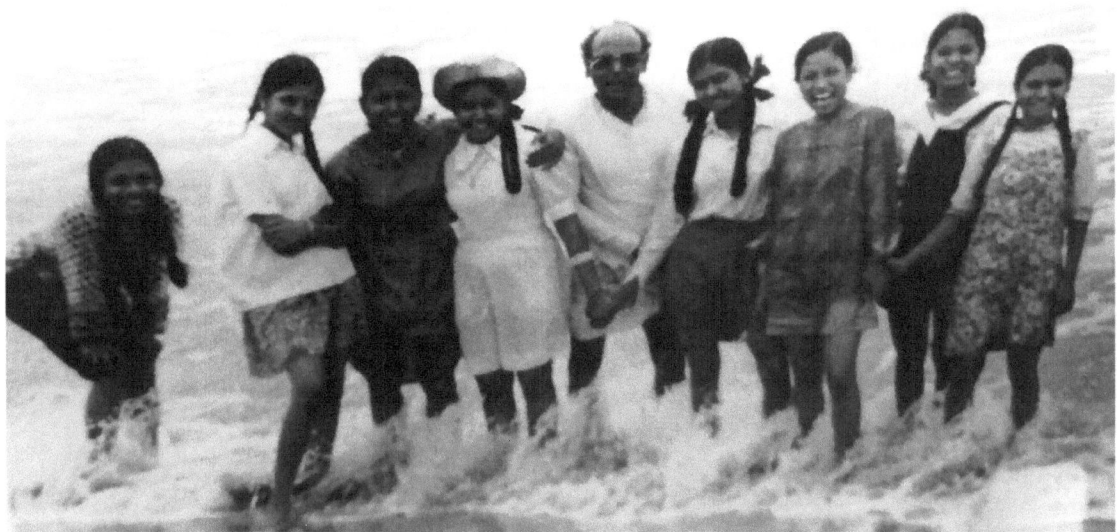

Enjoying Marina Beach, Chennai

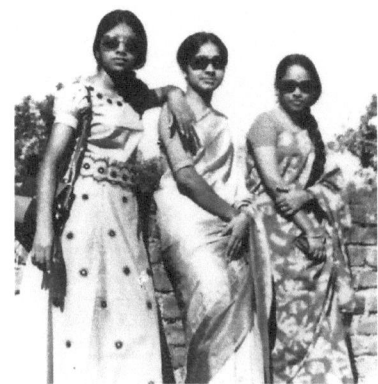

A visit to Indore

CHAPTER EIGHT

SABITA MISHRA

"Indian classical music and dance are not just for entertainment- they are designed to elevate your consciousness."

- Sadguru

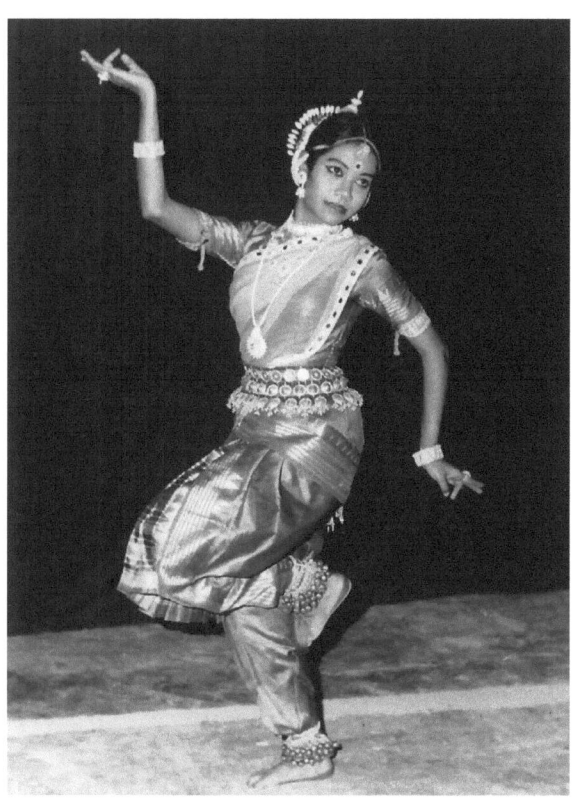

I joined KVK in the year 1966 when I was eight years old. Much against the wishes of my maternal grandfather, my mother introduced me to Odissi dance and encouraged me to attend classes in KVK. Though not interested in learning dance at that age I continued on mother's insistence. After two years I gradually developed interest and soon it became a passion. My father's dream of making me a doctor was shattered due to my obsession in dance. I was good at academics and would have done well in the med school but dance became my sole focus.

Following the six-year curriculum in the program of study, I went through a very methodical training in Odissi dance under gurus Raghunath Dutta and Ramani Ranjan Jena. It was the intensive summer training course under Guru Kelucharan Mohapatra, which helped refine my style, build stamina and perfect the technique. A lot of time was spent in the summer class in focusing on the finer aspects of the dance style. Similar to craftsmen who make fine filigree jewelry in Odisha, Guru Kelucharan Mohapatra worked for hours with each one of us to bring perfection in dance and precision in movements. I was a sincere student and learned both the practical and theory aspects of Odissi dance with equal zeal. Dr. Nilamadhab Bose was instrumental in providing a strong base in our knowledge of the theoretical aspects.

I enjoyed our dance tours and the time I spent with friends. Traveling for performances was like going for a picnic. Sometimes even when bus and train travel was rough, the joy of being together helped in overlooking it. Some of the most memorable trips were a month long tour to various cities in southern India, and a visit to the IAS and IFS Institute in Mussoorie and Dehradun. While in Etawah to participate in the annual program of Gandharva Sangeet Mahavidyalaya, we danced in freezing temperature. Being in the company of friends, the discomfort in travel or in extreme weather became inconspicuous. Nandita Behera,

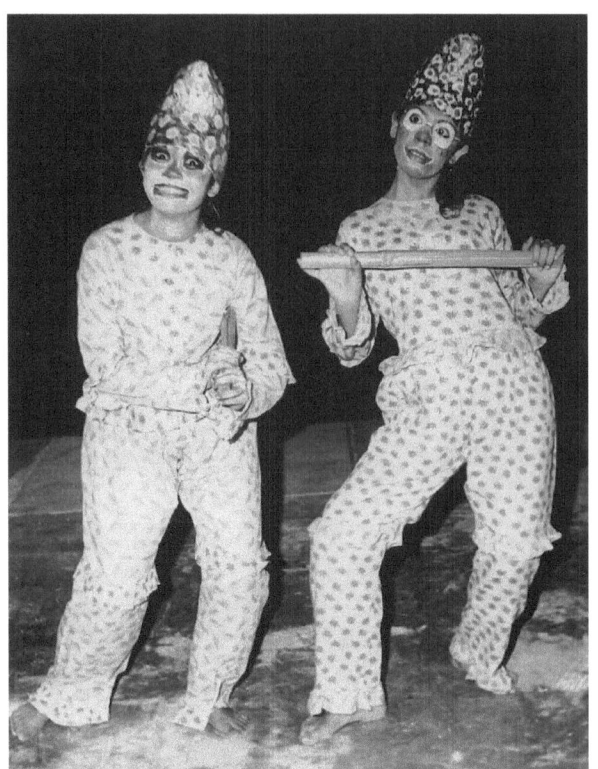

Sabita (Left) and Sikata (Right) in Circus

Sikata, Rohini and I danced together in many places and festivals. I was so glad that after so many years, we are reconnecting due to Rohini's efforts. We were together in the journey of learning dance and have so many memories of our times spent in KVK. It was more so enthralling to learn with my sister Salila though she was two years younger to me.

KVK, was the premier institution where the programs of study in dance, music and theatre was well planned and taught by legendary teachers. Visiting scholars and artists were the cherry on the top. For my friends and me, the methodical training spread through the years, enabled a strong foundation in Odissi dance. Besides, the experiences of travel and performances, pursuing dance education improved my social skills, opened opportunities to learn from and with others, explore diversity in language, food and finally be more tolerant of differences.

Though I had never planned to become a dance teacher, since the year 1990 I have been teaching Odissi dance in my studio at home. From the last eight years, I also offer lessons in Jharkhand Kala Mandir, Govt. of Jharkhand, Ranchi where I get the opportunity to share this dance form with Adivasi girls. My approach in training is to provide a wholesome process in learning, where both theory and practical lessons are given equal time and focus. My objective is to provide children the opportunity to learn and perform in the same way as I received from my teachers. A lot of students are receiving CCRT scholarships under my guidance. The Govt. of Jharkhand has honored me for my contributions in this field.

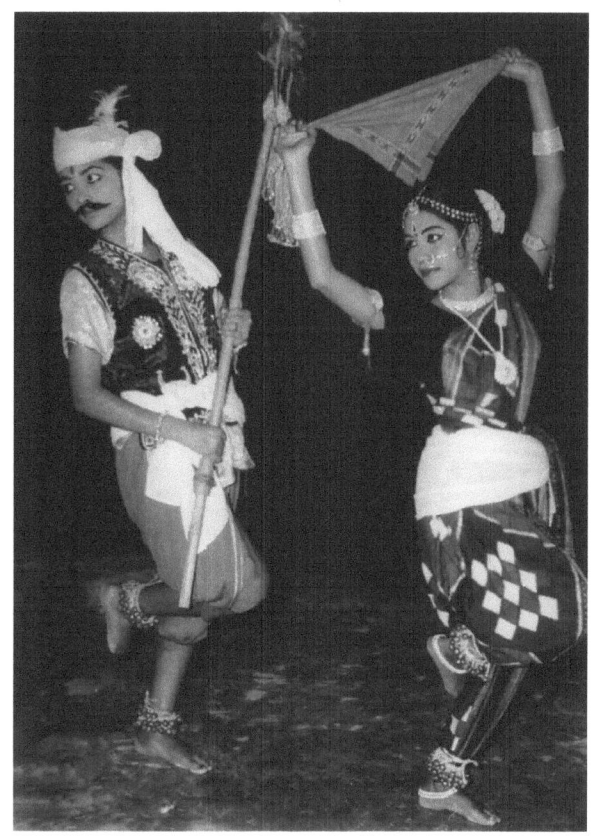

Nandita (Left) and Sabita (Right) in folk dance

I am grateful to Babulal Doshi, for his sincere and untiring efforts in establishing KVK, without which we would not have had such an enriching experience.

POST PERFORMANCE

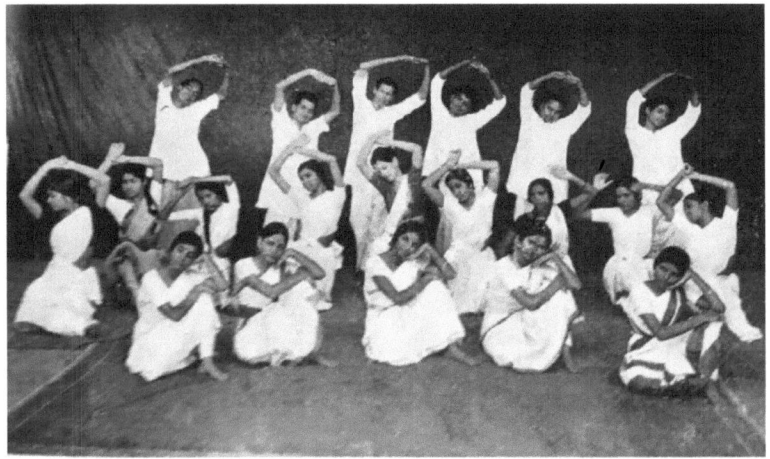

Participants of Intensive summer course at KVK

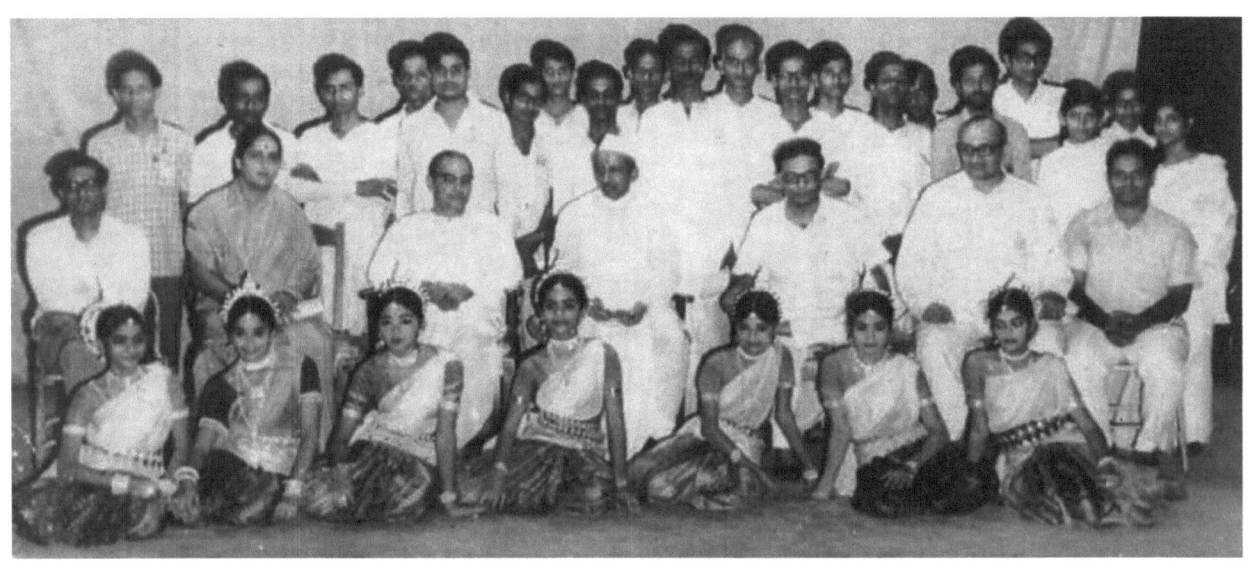

A visit by Vice President B.D. Jatti during the Sliver Jubilee celebrations

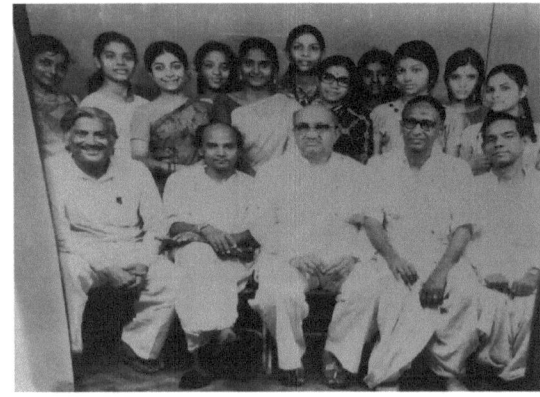

A visit to Vijayawada

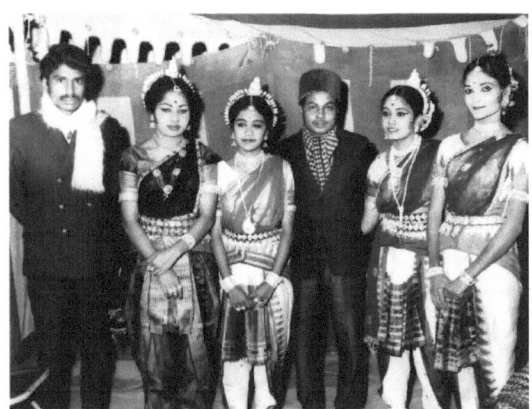

A visit to Etawah

CHAPTER NINE

PRABHAT NALINI MISRA

"To live is to dance, to dance is to live."
- Charles M. Schulz

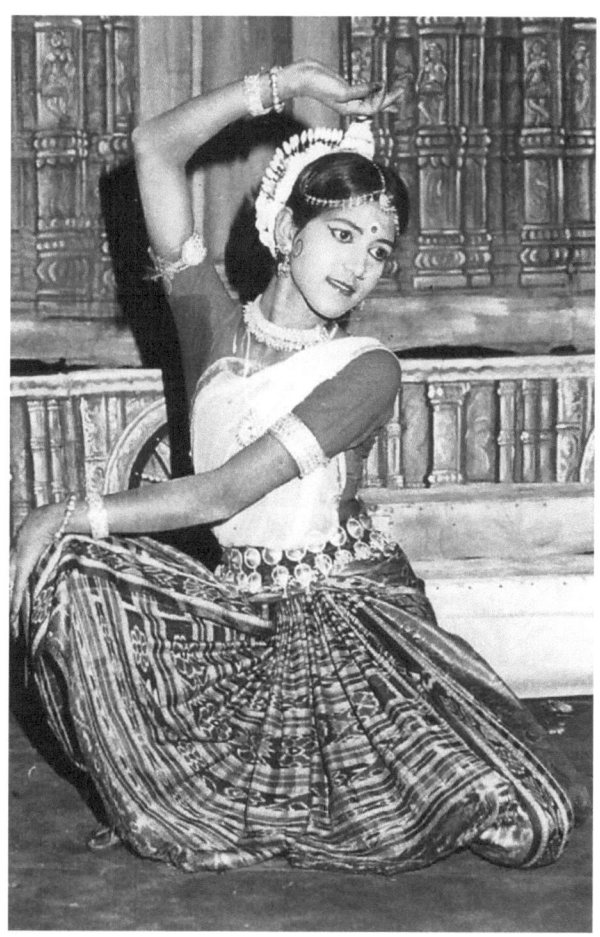

Dance means a lot to me, it is my first love, a passion and is the source of my inner satisfaction throughout my career and life.

Since the age of three, I have often danced to music playing on the radio. Seeing my passion, my parents arranged for me to learn dance under the tutelage of Guru Raghunath Dutta in a school of dance in our neighborhood. His devotion and my commitment helped in cultivating my inherent love for dance.

After few years of training and on completion of second year dance course, I joined KVK. Undoubtedly, KVK was the first and foremost premier institution of dance and once I joined there it was no looking back.

Under the guidance of several gurus, I earned the degree "Nritya Bhushan" on completion of six years of learning Odissi. Many opportunities came my way during this period when my friends and I performed in different parts of the country, sponsored by the state government or corporate institutions. Participation in these programs gave me immense pleasure and cannot be explained in words.

During my ten-year-long association with KVK, I learned discipline, punctuality, team spirit, control of body and mind, devotion, commitment and total involvement both on and of stage. My love for dance did not end with marriage. I continued to present Odissi dance on several occasions.

Last but not the least, my sincere heartfelt gratitude to my gurus, love and best wishes to my friends with whom I have spent long memorable golden moments. Given an opportunity again, I could go back to KVK with same spirit and enthusiasm to participate in more and more events till my last breath.

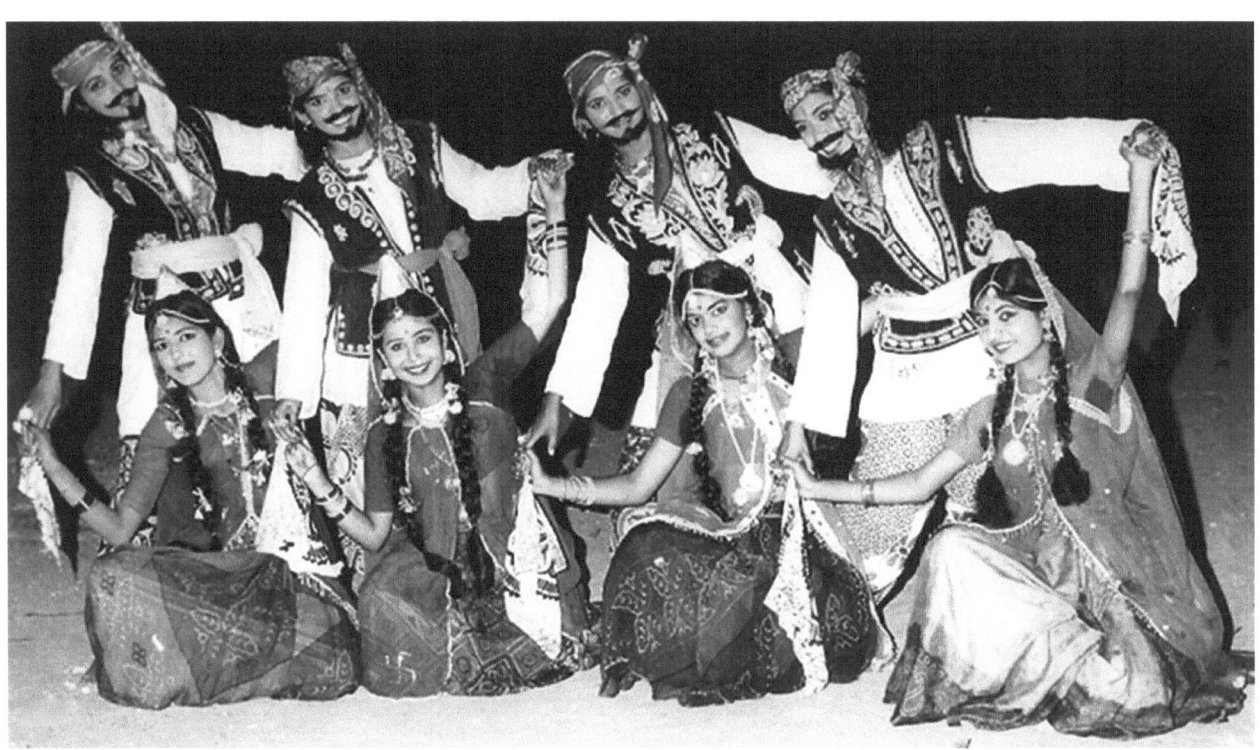

Prabhat Nalini (seated first left) in a folk dance

CHAPTER TEN

SIKATA MOHANTY

"Dancing is as old as love."

- Lucian

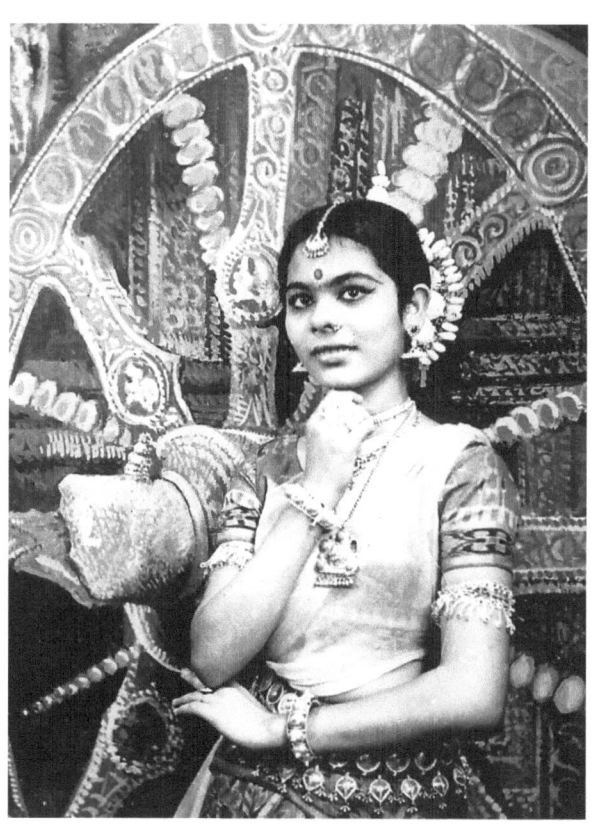

I stepped into this great institution to learn dance, some 52 years ago in 1965, at the age of five, even before my admission to a pre-nursery school. The same year, I got the rare opportunity to participate in a dance-drama "Krishna Leela" as Madumangala (a close friend of Krishna) and also as a calf. During that time, dance teachers in KVK were Guru Kelucharan Mohapatra, Guru Mayadhar Rout, Guru Ramani Ranjan Jena and Guru Raghunath Datta. These gurus rose to the highest level of excellence, won many laurels and brought fame for our country. At a young age, I was fortunate to be able to begin my training under their guidance and also share the stage with many other senior and junior dancers.

It is impossible to describe my complete experience and feelings of my days at Kala Vikash Kendra (KVK). However, I am making a modest attempt to share my experience.

I was 11 years old when I completed the sixth year in the study of dance. I was one of the youngest students appearing for the sixth year exam in dance so Kelu Sir came to our house and asked my father what to do if I passed. My father requested him to design my next phase in dance education.

I passed the sixth year exam in first division and Kelu Sir asked me to join the intensive training course held in the summer season., Dancers from various parts of world joined the two month long training program conducted by Kelu Sir. I attended the summer intensive training course for four consecutive years and passed the exams successfully in the first division. During this period I became close with many dancers visiting from various countries. Learning dance became an addiction.

We participated in many programs throughout the country. Rehearsals, the aroma of "one samosa- one black sweet" as refreshment was thrilling. And it was even more challenging and enjoyable to be able to convince the helper, Sanatan, to buy more samosa-sweets for distribution among friends!

KVK was about seven kilometers from my house and cycle-rickshaw was the only mode of travel for us. The long ride to the dance school began with being picked up at station bazaar, followed by halts for other friends at College Square, Mangalabag, Baniasahi, Buxibazar, then via YMCA road and finally reaching KVK. While returning, it was the same route, starting from KVK and I was the last to reach home. Especially during the winter season, bundled in woolens and a monkey cap, I would reach home late in the night, cold, hungry, and half asleep. As my home approached, Bolu, our favorite rickshaw-puller, would wake me up. En route to KVK, we packed different snacks like guava, berries, buxi bazar mixtures sprinkled with lemon juice and onions, and sometimes we also had candies and chocolates. The food, fun, and chit chatting was sheer pleasure during those days.

We also danced in the Odia cinemas "Adina Megha" and then in "Krishna Sudama''.

Listening to the melodious songs of Raghunanda Sir in music class is all still fresh in my memory. It was quite exciting to secretly peek back stage in the newly built auditorium of KVK , and sometimes also see the sets of the ongoing magic show of world famous magician P C Sircar.

The years of my childhood, adolescence, and some part of my youth I spent in KVK with my friends. It brought happiness, sorrow, anger, and innumerable other joyous experiences as we lived and danced together. Even today I clearly remember the thrill and excitement of those days and the various events we participated in.

In 1975 we toured the southern region of India for programs. While in Vijayawada I received the results of my matriculation examination. Earning first class was really exciting. I threw a party and we all celebrated together.

Kumar Utsav and Raja Utsav were the other highlights of that period. It used to be celebrated in a big way at Cuttack. KVK used to take the lead in presenting new and innovative dance dramas. I still remember my friends and our senior group of dancers. I feel privileged to have been part of these dance festivals.

Many dance dramas were choreographed by Kelu Sir and Raghu Sir at KVK. The dance drama "Circus" choreographed by Raghu Sir was staged a number of times and I used to dance as Nartaki. It was amusing to dance clad in mini skirt and blouse with a dafali in hand. On other occasions Sabita and I played the role of jokers. We made people laugh with our funny acts and caricatures. Nandita and Rohini played the role of the circus master and his wife. During that period, renowned maestros such as Balakrushna Sir, Rakhal Sir, Bhikari Bal Sir used to sing and Bhubaneswar Sir used to compose the music and play the violin.

More than five decades have passed, and I have grown to be a performer, trainer, choreographer, and a researcher, and have received many accolades. I treasure the memories of my dance school KVK and the friends I made while learning dance. In 2012 during KVK's Diamond Jubilee celebration I was felicitated and I also performed. Immediately after my performance, Nilu Da came to the stage , hugged me and said "In you we found Kelu Babu. As if he is dancing not Sikata". It was a home coming for me. Memories of the cherished moments in KVK will be with me for times to come.

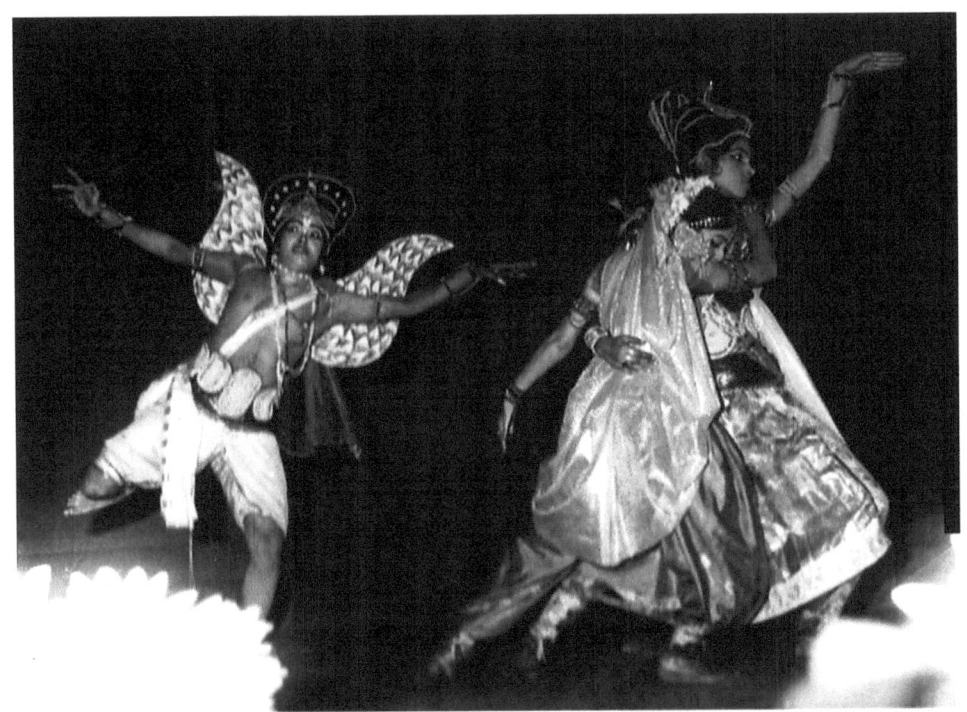

Scene from dance drama "Amar Prem"

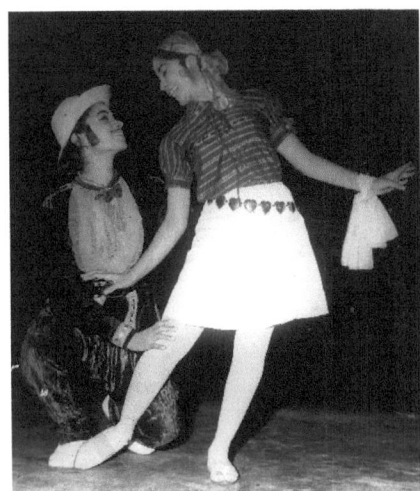

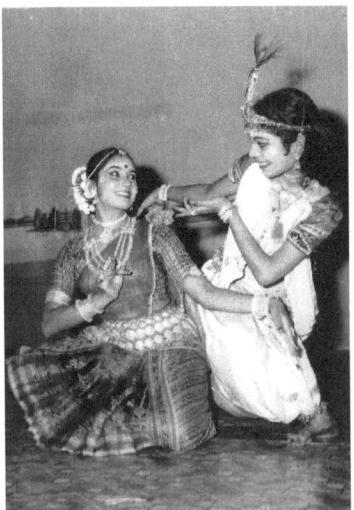

Nandita and Rohini in "Circus"

Sikata and Rohini in "Geet Govind"

Sabita and Rohini in "Dashavatar"

CHAPTER ELEVEN

PRANATI MOHANTY

"Dancing is like dreaming with your feet."
- *Constanze Mozart*

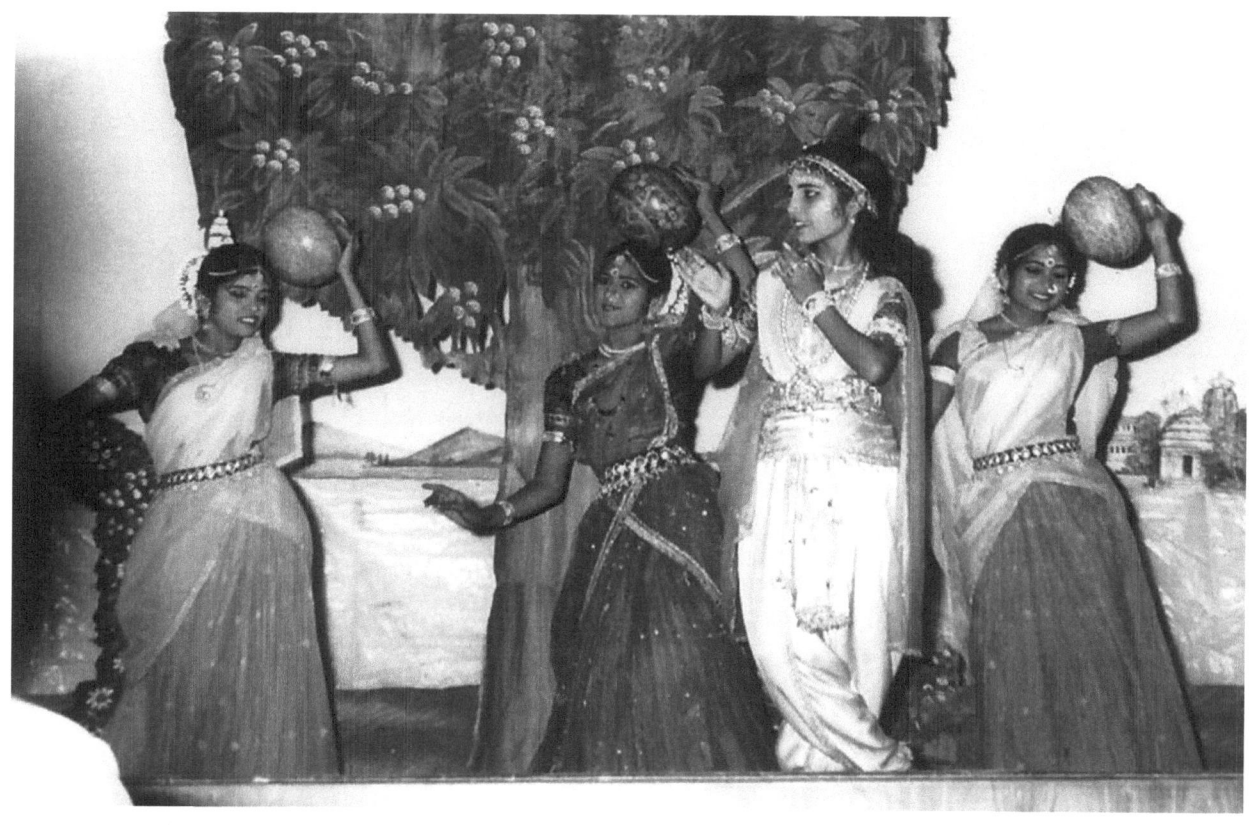

Pranati as Krishna in the dance drama Krishna Gatha

In the year 1969 at the age of eight, I was admitted to KVK for formal training in Odissi dance. I spent approximately 11 years in KVK, learning Odissi dance. My teachers were Ramani Ranjan Jena, Raghunath Dutta, and Kelucharan Mohapatra. For a brief period of two months I also took lessons with Guru Mayadhar Raut. I remember all these gurus, for their dedication and sincerity in training students.

Looking back, I treasure several memorable moments. During my initial years of dance training in KVK, I used to be scared of late Raghunath Dutta, so I skipped most of his classes. Due to my frequent absences from his classes, a message was conveyed to my parents from KVK, after which I was forced to attend those classes. As I resumed my classes, I learned that KVK was preparing for the Silver Jubilee celebrations. And because I had missed so many classes of my course, I was not given a chance to participate. This incident opened my eyes and I began attending class regularly. Seeing all my classmates busy with dance rehearsals without me made me very sad. However, one day during the period of rehearsals, one of the students declined to perform for personal reasons, and as a result I was given the opportunity to perform on stage. This incident became the turning point of my life.

On another occasion, we traveled to Bhillai for a program and were scheduled to present the dance drama, Krishna Gatha. Rohini apa was playing the role of Sri Krishna and I was playing the role of a Gopi. On the very day of the performance, Rohini apa fell ill and could not perform, so Raghu Sir asked me if I could take her place. Without any hesitation I accepted the challenge. After the performance, Babulal Doshi (Babu bhai) walked up to me with praises and thanked me for accepting such a difficult task. That was the most memorable moment of my life.

Last but not the least, during my sixth year, KVK honored me with the award "Pratima Dash," a trophy, which boosted my confidence as a performer.

Late Padmabibhushan Kelucharan Mohapatra also contributed in the development of my dance career. He promoted me on various platforms. One of them was "National Scholarship" and the award "Sringarmani" which was presented by Sur Sringar Sansad Mumbai, in the year 1981. Presently, I continue to teach Odissi dance in my school at Angul, Odisha. Lessons in Odissi dance in KVK has taught me the essence of life and I have learned that there is no short cut to achieving success.

DR. SUMITRA MOHAPATRA

"Let this day be lost to us on which we did not dance once."
- Friedrich Nietzsche

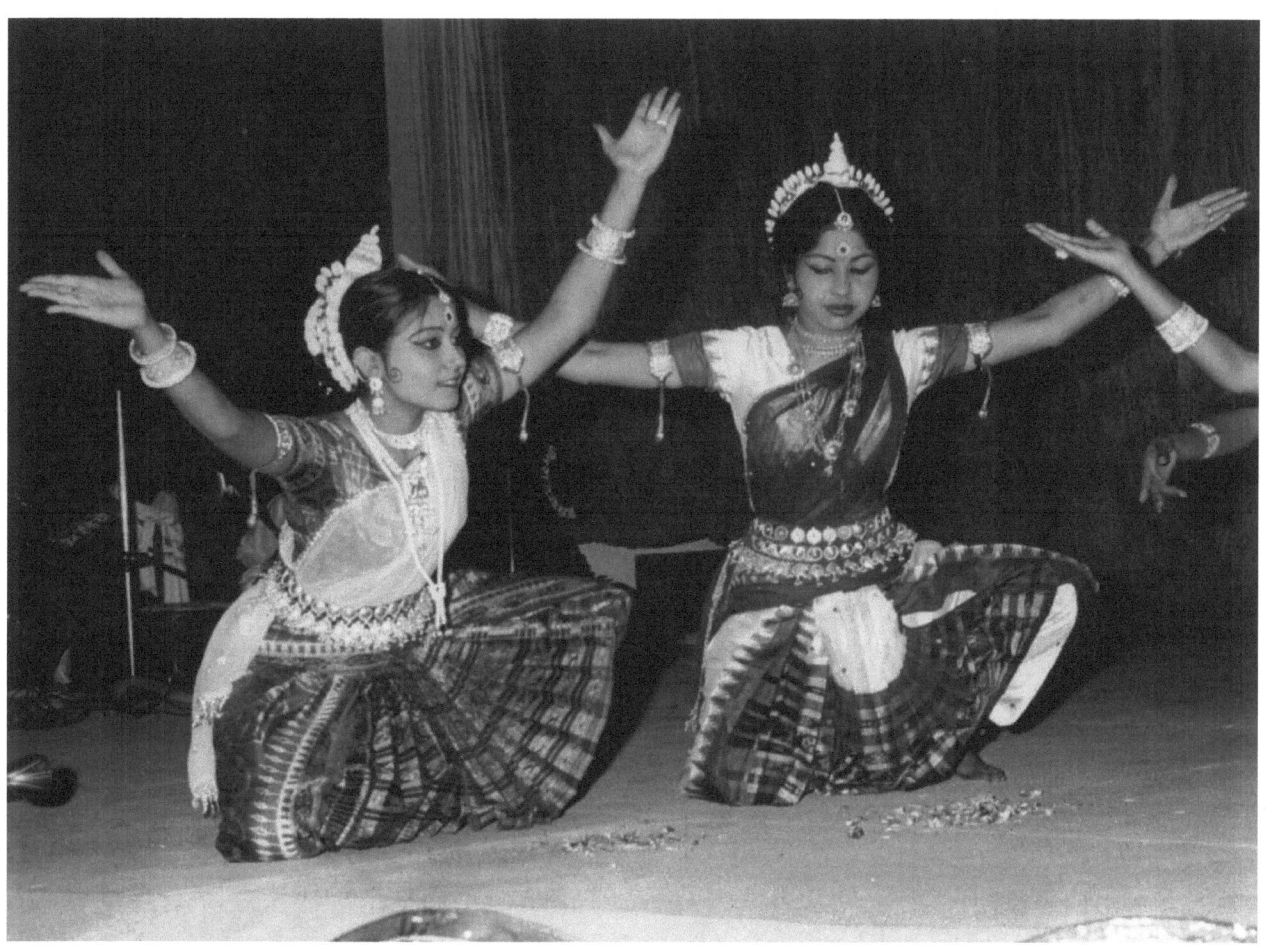

Sumitra (right) with Rohini performing in Etawah

Life moves on and time gone never comes back. Though that is the reality, the journey of one's life and experiences become treasured memories. As I reminisce the time I spent in Kala Vikash Kendra (KVK), I relive those priceless moments and events that have contributed to making my life beautiful.

I am now sharing those precious moments, when I was learning Odissi dance and became one of the top Odissi dancers of the famous dance institute Kala Vikash Kendra. I was trained under the tutelage of famous gurus, namely Guru Kelucharan Mohapatra, Guru Raghunath Dutta and Guru Ramani Ranjan Jena.

I joined the Odissi dance program of study, which spanned six years, after which I received the degrees of Nritya Visharad and Nritya Praveen. Under the direction of the Founder, Shri Babulal Doshi, gurus and students continued to receive immense support and encouragement. We were offered many opportunities to experience and learn the beautiful dance form. Babulal Doshi's dedication to the arts of Odisha is immeasurable. He gave us a platform to showcase our talents and participate in many national and international dance & music festivals in India and abroad.

A three-month-long intensive summer workshop held in KVK during summer was conducted by Guru Kelucharan Mohapatra. This workshop brought together the intermediate level and senior students, other upcoming gurus, and students from outside of Odisha. It was a rich

learning experience and we had the privilege of sharing the class with famous dancers like Kumkum Mohanty, Rani Karna, Sonal Mansingh, Maneka Thakkar and my dear friend Protima Bedi. We got the opportunity to observe these famous dancers during class lessons and build relationships with the visiting dancers, which we continue to cherish.

In the sixth year of my training, while I was working towards earning my degree of Nrutya Praveen, I received the National Scholarship for Dance from the Department of Culture of the Government of India. KVK became my second home. Long hours of rehearsals and classes consumed my days and balancing my academic pursuit became challenging.

The fun times for us were when we had rehearsals for the annual programs and during our convocation. We practically lived in KVK. Kelu Sir used to be very stressed during final stage rehearsal on the night before the show. All dancers musicians, light and stage technicians were not allowed to go home. Those were our sleepless days and nights.

I value this phase of my life. Words cannot express my love and gratitude towards KVK. It provided us the right platform and support, motivated us along the path to progress in our chosen field of work under the guidance of scholars and able gurus. I received the valuable experience of being deeply involved in the rich cultural heritage of the state of Odisha, the place of my birth. It can be said that during the 70s and 80s KVK was the "happening" place of the arts in Odisha. Writing this piece led me to retrace my life and it was great reliving those precious and treasured moments, which I am more than happy to share with all.

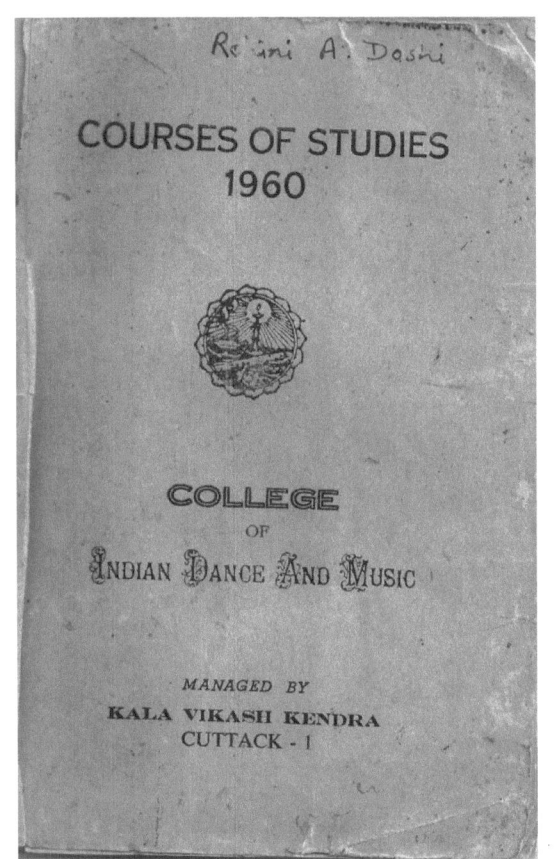

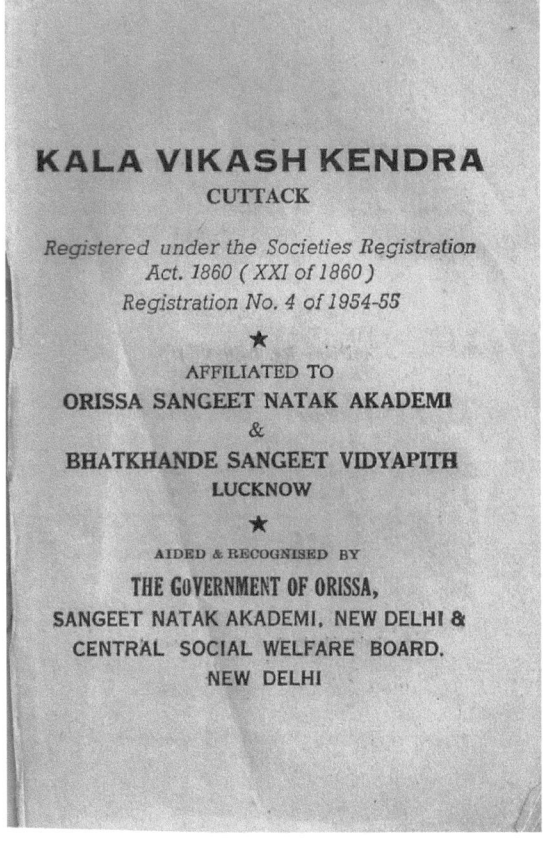

CHAPTER THIRTEEN

SANGEETA MAHAPATRA KAR

"Dance is your pulse, your heartbeat, your breathing. It's the rhythm of your life. It's the expression in time and movement, in happiness, joy, sadness and envy."

- Jacques d' Amboise

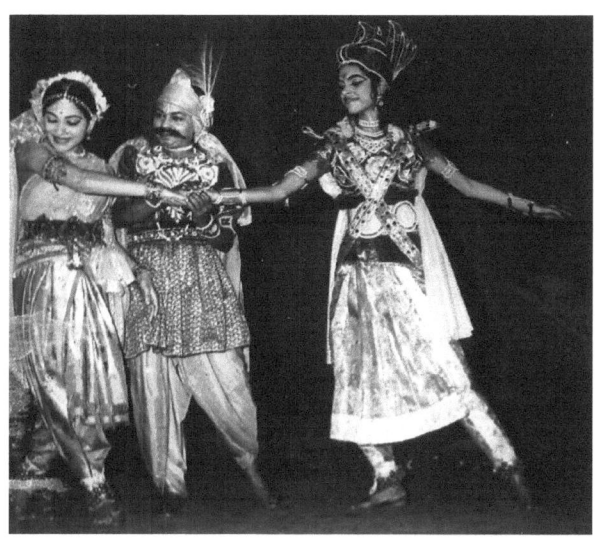

Sangeeta (right) with Cuckoomeena (left) and Guru Raghunath Datta (middle) in the dance drama Amar Prem.

I was fortunate to have started learning Odissi dance from Guru Kelucharan Mohapatra at my house since the age of 3. I remember Sir (that is what we used to call Guruji) used to reward me with orange candies if I did my steps right. After few years he asked my mom to enroll me in Kala Vikash Kendra (KVK) where he was teaching, as it was important for me to learn in a formal program of study. This continued for several years, private lessons from Guruji and group lessons in KVK where I was also taught by Raghu Sir and Ramani Sir.

Apart from dance lessons, I participated in several dance dramas and the fun part was the rehearsals and adorning ourselves with special dance drama accessories like crowns, costumes and ornaments. I also enjoyed the KVK rickshaw rides where the students used to be picked up from their homes.

I remember at the end of each lesson in KVK, Guruji used to make us all sit down and write what we learned that day starting with "Aaji classer aame … sikhilu"(Today we learned…).

I earned my degree of Nritya Bhushan from KVK and performed all over India. On moving to the United States after marriage, I started an institute of Odissi dance and Hindusthani classical music and have taught more than 600 students. Besides dance, I learned to sing and received the degree of Sangeet Alankar in Hindusthani classical vocal music under Guru Deepak Basu from Gandharva Mahavidyalaya Mandal. I received both Singar Mani and Surmani awards from Sur Singar Samsad in Mumbai.

I have learned many things from Guruji but the one thing I treasure the most is Guruji's eye for detail in choreography. He also had an natural sense of music and in fact used to sing and play the mardal when we danced. Listening to him play the mardal and sing has helped me a lot. Especially when I choreographed the 11 dance dramas with 50 plus dancers each time.

Dance and music have played a very significant part in my life especially as I am so far away from my birth country. Apart from imparting Indian culture, Odissi dance has maintained my physical health and music my mental. Both have contributed to enrich my soul and develop a positive attitude. Being in the company of my students and their families almost on a daily basis, I have been blessed with a general feeling of well being. I feel grateful for the guidance I received from my gurus and the opportunities that came my way due to my association with KVK.

TIKLIMEENA PATNAIK

"Let us read and let us dance. These two amusements will never do any harm to this world."

- Voltaire

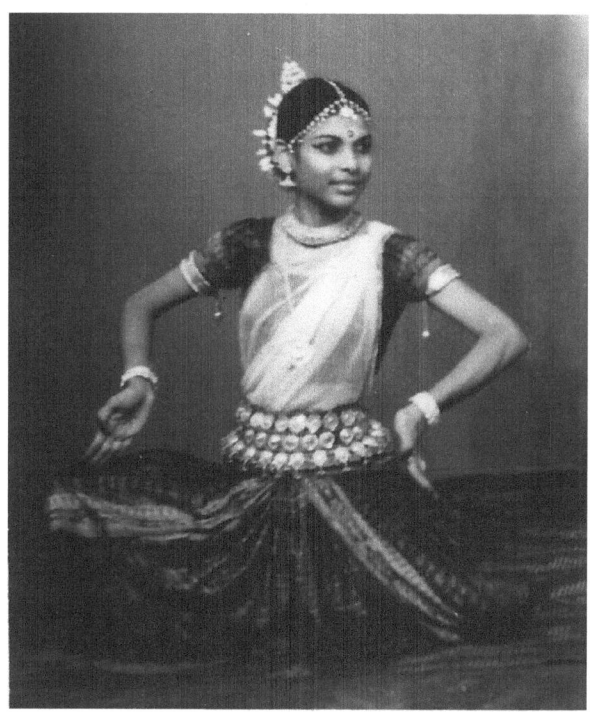

KVK is the pioneer institute in classical Odissi dance, song, and instrumental music. I had the opportunity to learn Odissi dance when I was 5 years old. I was admitted to Prarambhik and went through rigorous training under the guidance of Guru Kelu Charan Mohapatra, Guru Mayadhar Raut,

Guru Raghunath Dutt and Guru Ramani Ranjan Jena. I graduated from the six year program and then attended the four years of summer intensive classes, followed by further training with Guru Kelu Charan Mohapatra and Guru Ramani Ranjan Jena until I moved to the United States.

My parents believed that learning dance and music was important in human development and so they encouraged me and my siblings to engage in dance and music. I am the youngest among the four children. Cuckoomeena, my older sister was an accomplished Odissi dancer; Chiku Meena, my second older sister learned to play the violin and guitar; and my brother Sri Gopal also pursued the arts.

I feel fortunate today because besides learning dance, I could bond with my friends forever. This truly is a blessing for me. Although we learned our discipline, manners, and values at home and school, KVK had its share in molding us as good citizens and above all taught us the importance of working hard in life.

KVK was not just a dance school for me, but was a place where we danced, played, and bonded. Those sweet memories of our childhood have been imprinted in my life forever. After so many years, I still remember several of my good friends. Their love, affection and laughter, are treasured in my heart. Learning dance in KVK was a big opportunity, which I hardly realized when I was young. Babulal Doshi's efforts did not go in vain. Odissi dance is now known all over the world.

I was sincere in learning dance and wanted to be a dance teacher. When famous dancers like Sanjukta Panigrahi, Kumkum Das, and Cuckoo Meena used to learn dance, I always admired them and wanted to be a great dancer like them. Having said that, it was not always easy for me because I was 5 feet 6 inches tall and very slim. In those days people had a notion that an Odissi dancer should be average in height (shorter than me). So our Gurus were always in a dilemma when it came to choosing an

appropriate role for me in dance dramas. But this outlook changed when students from outside of Odisha and foreign countries came to learn Odissi dance. Some of those dancers are Protima Bedi, Sharon Lowen and Ileana Citaristi. When I was in the intensive classes in summer, Guru Kelu Charan Mohapatra would make me stand in the front row because I remembered the dances well.

My other good memory of KVK was the fun time I had with friends on the swing sets, the singing, and playing in the small park in the sweet lingering fragrance of the night queen flowers. To date, as I visualize that image, I hear the laughter and sense the sweet smell. The camaraderie alongside dance lessons was an extraordinary experience of my life and holds a special place in my heart.

My special thanks go first to Madhu Chhanda (Chumki) for posting a group picture on Face Book, which inspired us to share our memories. Secondly, I thank my dear friend Dr. Rohini Dandavate for her efforts in documenting those beautiful times spent together in KVK. Learning Odissi dance truly changed our lives forever.

CHAPTER FIFTEEN

DR. NANDITA SEN

"Dance is for everybody. I believe that the dance came from the people and that it should always be delivered back to the people."

- Alvin Ailey

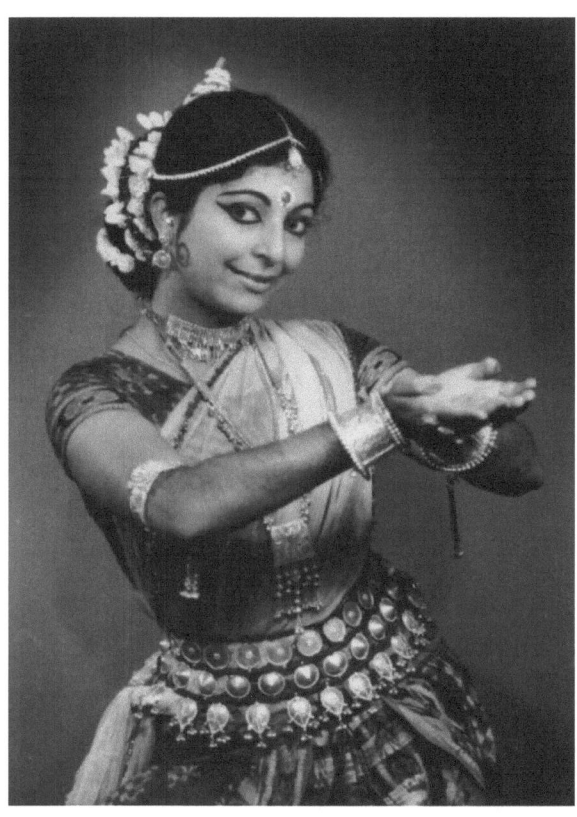

I received a phone call from Rohini Doshi, my School junior and an Odissi dancer, who took me down memory lane.

My family had moved into our grandparents home in Cuttack during the later half of 1963 since my father was posted to a field area, being an Infantry Officer of the Armed Forces. It was my father's desire that I learn this dance form, for its encompassing glory of grace, devotion, and enlightenment. With this back drop, I took baby steps into Odissi in 1964. I was homeschooled by my first Guru Shri Raghunath Dutta .

In 1966, I enrolled in the hallowed precincts of Kala Vikash Kendra, fondly called 'KVK', an institution where the likes of its founder Shri Babulal Doshi and Odissi gurus like Padmashri Guru Kelu Charan Mohapatra, Guru Ramani Ranjan Jena, and Guru Raghunath Dutta were painstakingly involved in taking Odissi to its' well deserved level on the international stage. It became an all-consuming passion. Under the ardent tutelage of all three Gurujis, I blossomed into a tiny, avid Odissi dancer. It was such a coincidence that eventually my father got posted to

Cuttack and we were allotted our Government residential Quarters right opposite Kala Vikash Kendra. Life for me was ecstatic with school in the morning and running to 'KVK' for dance classes in the evening. The rhythmic beats of the mardal along with the accompanying heart warming music from KVK were an all pervasive magnetic pull.

Years simply flew by with simultaneous exacting schedules of theory and practical lessons culminating in the prestigious award of Nritya Bhushan in Odissi in the year 1969 to make my family joyfully proud. There are no words to express my gratitude to this great Institution, Kala Vikash Kendra, and my three Gurujis in giving me this life changing experience. It was sheer revelry, rigorous dance practice, and performing for months together, travelling to numerous destinations; it was a constant learning experience. Sharing the stage with Sanjukta Panigrahi in Padmashri Guru Kelucharan Mohapatra's 'Geeta Govinda' and 'Konarka' with Shri Raghunath Panigrahi's melodious music composition, in the seventies (as a young Medical student), was sheer happiness all the way.

I eventually became a doctor, to fulfill another dream of my parents. Now in the twilight years of my life, I cherish so many fond memories of my growing up dancing years.

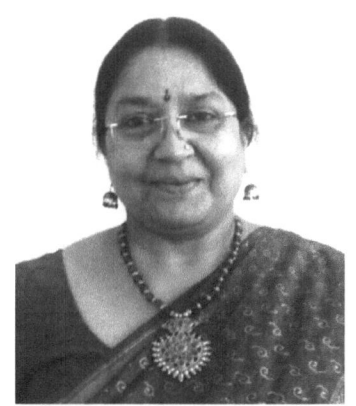

ABOUT THE EDITOR

Dr. Rohini Dandavate holds a doctoral degree in Cultural Policy and Arts Administration from The Ohio State University. She received training in Odissi dance in Kala Vikash Kendra, Cuttack from Guru Kelucharan Mohapatra, Guru Raghunath Dutta, Guru Ramani Ranjan Jena, and Dr. Menaka Thakkar.

Rohini's work spans the areas of dance performance, arts administration, art education and cultural policy. She produces multimedia learning resources for home practice and reference. These resources are available online on Createspace.com, an Amazon company. She also writes papers and articles which discuss issues in dance education, arts administration and cultural policy. Prior to this, as an artist in the Arts Learning Program of the Ohio Arts Council, Rohini conducted Odissi dance workshops and lecture demonstrations for students and audiences in educational and community institutions. Her projects are designed to provide audiences a window to observe, explore and relate to diverse cultures through the experience of the arts.